GERD LUDWIG

My
Rat

BARRON'S

CONTENTS

5   Proper Care and Good Health

6   Learning, Playing, and Keeping Busy

Reproduction and Rearing

What to Do When There Are Problems

Appendix

What Rats
Are Like

Rats have a wide variety of behavioral strategies that they use to hold their own in practically every situation in life. In the process they have always sought proximity to humans.

World Citizens and Masters of Adaptation

Rats are curious, crafty, hardy, and prolific. They feel secure in the pack: They search for food together and fight against intruders—the best measures for coping with all situations in life.

A RAT IS NEVER ALONE. Rats are powerful and very clever creatures that can use their teeth as impressive defensive tools in an emergency. But a rat gets its strength and security only from association with others of its kind: the pack.

The Family Is Everything

Wild brown rats live in large groups of twenty to sixty, or even more. Because most of the pack members are related to each other, a rat pack is a family association.

▶ Communication in the pack is based on complex body and vocal language (see page 21) and chemical communication. This guarantees orderly dealings in the group and avoids misunderstandings.

▶ Family members recognize one another by a specific pack smell: Every rat that smells differently is attacked and driven away.

▶ The pack has a territory that is delineated with scent markings and defended against intruders.

▶ Males establish territories with several females.

▶ Pack members search for food together and explore unfamiliar territory.

▶ Rats build living and sleeping places in their territory, construct passageways, and raise their young to adulthood.

▶ Rats need to be with others of their kind. Rats that live alone waste away.

Nosy and On Guard

Rats are curious—and they are cautious. Like few other animals, rats have learned to combine these two opposite characteristics and use them for their benefit. Next to searching for food sources, curiosity is a strong impetus for discovery (exploration behavior) that has

Curiosity and a strong urge to explore are characteristic of rats. They love to inspect unfamiliar territory and objects in twos or threes.

allowed the rodents to colonize nearly every habitat in the world—usually in the wake of humans. For example, many rats (mostly house rats) departed as unwitting passengers on long voyages by ship. It's not a rat's style to announce, "Here I come!" In case of doubt, unforeseen situations and possibly risky actions are avoided. The pack prefers to wait until the way is clear, or to search for reliable, alternative ways. This also applies to getting food. In the wild, rats generally steer a wide berth around unfamiliar food sources, and have developed strategies for minimizing risks (see page 75). Their relatives in the pet realm, who are descendants of laboratory rats (see page 14) and have been living for many generations under the protection of humans, act much more trusting and even accept strange food without hesitating very long.

Mouse Relatives

Rats are rodents. In the group of rodents (order of Rodentia), the true rats of the genus *Rattus* are classified among the mice (Muridae), the most numerous family of mammals with 300 genera and 1,336 species. There are about 50 species in the *Rattus* genus.
A Secretive Life. Followers of civilization such as brown rats and house rats are distributed worldwide. Most of the predominantly indigenous rat species in eastern and southeastern Asia live so secretly that even today the precise

1 **The house rat** is rarely encountered and is on the list of seriously endangered animal species. In Asia it remains a major threat to crops.

2 **The brown rat** is less choosy about places to live than the house rat. It has colonized all habitats on earth in the wake of humans and asserted itself over indigenous species.

Rats are omnivores, but they ▶
prefer grains and fruits.

number of species remains unknown. But so far more than 570 different forms have been described.

Mouse or Rat? Generally we understand mice to be house mice (*Mus musculus*), but *rat* designates the house rat *Rattus rattus* or the brown rat *Rattus norvegicus*. But taxonomically both genera, those of the mice and the rats, belong to the subfamily of the true mice. The common distinction thus refers more to the difference in size: Animals with a body length of more than 6 inches (15 cm) are generally considered to be rats, and those smaller are considered mice.

Brown Rats Are One Step Ahead

House Rats. House rats are unsurpassed as climbers—a heritage from their original life in trees. But this ability has not been much help in association with us: In some countries the house rat is nearly extinct and is on the list of seriously endangered animal species. One reason may be their preference for dry, warm dwelling places. Formerly, storehouses, barns, and open attics provided them with enough hiding places, but such refuges are rare today. But in Asia, house rats still play a prominent role. There they regularly destroy crops and supplies or make themselves intolerable to humans (see pages 13–14).

Brown Rats. Brown rats place no high demands on their food. In contrast to house rats, which eat seeds and fruits almost exclusively, brown rats also consume small amounts of animal food, for example from mice, birds, and other small animals that they can overpower. The fact that brown rats are so widely distributed is ascribable primarily to their ability to use practically every imaginable habitat—from drainage pipes and landfills to cellars and ditches. The animals usually remain close to the ground, since they prefer moist places and proximity to water.

The brown rat came to Central Europe from its original homeland in Central Asia and Northern China around the year 1000—considerably later than the house rat, whose existence in the Mediterranean area as early as the Ice Age has been verified. The brown rat got its misleading scientific name *Rattus norvegicus* at a time when people were convinced that the little rodents had come from Scandinavia.

Competitors for Habitat. House and brown rats are distributed throughout the entire world, and in many countries they live side by side. Even though the ecological requirements of both species are different (see above), *Rattus rattus* was increasingly driven from appropriate ground-level habitats and lower floors by *Rattus norvegicus*.

On the Trail of Humans

Like many other rat species, house and brown rats are typical followers of civilization that appear wherever humans take up residence—often shortly after or simultaneously with initial settlement. The brown rat puts its outstanding swimming and diving abilities to good use, and rivers and small lakes pose no obstacles.

Stowaways. Rats crossed large bodies of water as stowaways on board merchant ships; they reached the coasts of distant lands and even isolated islands.

Reproductive rates and adaptability make the rat a model of success. ◀

This is how rats (primarily house rats) made it to North America in 1755. The clever traveling companions were anything but welcome among humans, for they perceptibly reduced crop yields, decimated or contaminated supplies, and communicated various diseases.

Displacement of Indigenous Species. The appearance of the new residents was far worse for the indigenous animal species: They were not ready for the adaptable and prolific thieves. In the last two hundred years some twenty-two species of mammals have become extinct on the Australian continent—more than anywhere else on earth. Non-indigenous species are not free from blame in this development: In addition to cats and foxes, rats have played a decisive role. On many small islands in the tropics and subtropics most ground-nesting bird species disappeared shortly after rats arrived on the islands. The birds had no defense or flight strategies to defend themselves against the rodents.

Early Rodents in Australia. Teeth that researchers found in excavations in 1997 in Queensland prove that the rats that migrated on ships from Europe were not the first rodents on the fifth continent: The two-million-year-old teeth belonged to a tree mouse that is considered one of the ancestors of our mice and rats.

A Paradise for Rats. The way our modern houses are built and the branching plumbing systems of large cities provide ideal living conditions, especially for brown rats. Leftover food is disposed of in wastewater; garbage containers behind fast-food and drive-in restaurants are full to overflowing; and around railroad tracks and subway

A COMPARISON OF HOUSE AND BROWN RATS

CHARACTERISTIC	HOUSE RAT	BROWN RAT
Form	Slender, length head to rump 6–9 inches (16–22 cm), large and nearly naked ears, tail always longer than body; weight 2½–10 ounces (70–300 g)	Relatively plump, head to rump length 8–10 inches (20–26 cm), tail generally shorter than body; weight 6–18 ounces (180–500 g), males sometimes more
Color	Primarily dark gray (referred to as *black rat*), but also black, sometimes with white chest	Back and sides usually brownish gray, underside dirty white, some black animals
Food	Preferably seeds and fruits, animal protein generally only as a supplement	Omnivores, also accept animal food; the brown rat is also good at catching fishes
Reproduction	Gestation period 24 days, usually 6–12, 8 on average, but also up to 20 young, which come into the world naked and blind; (altricial animals)	Gestation period 20–24 days, numbers similar to house rat; altricial; males are ready to mate at 3 months, females a little later
Lifestyle	Primarily nocturnal lifestyle, likes to climb; prefers dry habitats; often in trees and upper levels in buildings (roof rats)	Active at dusk and at night, but also on the move during the day; earth dwellers that accept nearly all types of accommodations, preferably near water

TRAIT	THINGS WORTH KNOWING ABOUT RATS
Teeth	Rats don't lose their baby teeth.
Feet	Front feet have four toes (vestigial thumb); rear legs have five.
Sense of Smell	The Jacobson Organ in the roof of the mouth detects scents.
Heart	The heart rate is between 280 and 450 beats per minute.

A Harmonious Community

▶ 1 **Closeness Desired** For a rat the pack is the focus of life. Because of the complex system of communication there are rarely any misunderstandings or conflicts.

▶ 2 **Mealtimes** A rat goes to the food dish several times a day. But it always has just a small snack.

▶ 3 **Games and Sports** Only a sleeping rat remains motionless; otherwise movement is the order of the day, preferably in the company of other rats.

shafts there are countless hiding places from which the pack can begin its wanderings. People used to estimate populations as "one rat per resident," but this formula has long since become passé. In Mumbai alone, the former Bombay, there are about a billion rats; for New York the estimate is sixteen million, or two rats per inhabitant. Things are probably comparable in other large cities. Brown rats are rare only in places where the most recent accomplishments in architecture and city planning are not yet completed. So their presence in such places as Africa is limited principally to large and port cities.

Thermo-Outfit. The fact that rats are found in both cold and hot areas is because of, among other things, their tail. It is not only used for holding and balancing, but is also important in heat control. In the heat, special blood vessels channel the excess warmth away; in the cold, they contract and protect against heat loss.

A Long and Adventurous History

Rats have sought contact with people for thousands of years. In every regard this is an astonishing and extraordinary behavior, as even Grimek's *Animal Life* (volume 11) notes: ". . . this need to establish a connection is one of the most salient traits of rats; no other mammalian genus has it to such a pronounced degree."

Humans have played a central role in the history of certain rat species. At many times our own history certainly would have developed differently without the omnipresence of rats.

Worldwide Culture Followers

House and brown rats are the only two rat species that have joined up with humans in North America. Especially in Asia, many additional representatives of the more than fifty species of the comprehensive genus *Rattus* that live in proximity to humans are known: the

fruit rat *Rattus rattus frugivorus*, the rice paddy rat, *R. argentiventer*, the Pacific rat *R. exulans*, the Malayan house rat *R. rattus diardii*, the Turkistan rat *R. rattoides*, the Himalayan rat *R. nitidus*, and a few others.

Rats as Disease Carriers

Rodents living in the wild can communicate diseases and act as intermediate hosts for pathogens. With rats this applies to such diseases as tuberculosis, typhus, cholera, and dysentery, as well as bubonic plague, whose epidemic character has been known ever since antiquity. It wasn't until 1894 that the French scientist Alexandre Yersin and the Japanese Shibasaburo Kitasato discovered the pathogen that causes plague, the bacterium *Yerisina pestis.* Three years later the rat flea *Xenopsylla cheopis* fell under suspicion as a carrier. It migrates to humans when the host animal dies from the pestilence. Nowadays plague can be treated with medications; however, it has not been eliminated. According to recent reports there were fourteen outbreaks in five countries from 2001 to 2006.

The Black Death

Between 1347 and 1351 more than twenty-three million people succumbed to the "black death." However, this probably was not a plague epidemic. For one thing, there were hardly any brown rats in Europe at the time, and house rats lived only in the Mediterranean region.

TIP

For a Better Image

Help to reduce prejudices against rats and to improve their image. Rats are dirty: On the contrary, they are exceedingly clean. Rats communicate diseases: This does not apply to pet rats. Rats are aggressive: They are peaceable in a pack and loving toward humans.

Also the epidemic spread more quickly than is typical for the plague. There is lots of evidence that the worst epidemic in human history was caused by a viral infection similar to the Ebola fever.

Protected, Revered, and Pampered

Especially in Asian cultures, rats are admired and revered, and considered as bringers of good luck. The Indian god India; they are protected and coddled with treats by believers. Particularly good fortune befalls visitors to the temple if a white rat crosses their path.

The Chinese calendar contains twelve animal signs (earthly branches). According to legend, Buddha had invited all the animals to a New Year's party, but only twelve accepted his invitation: rat, cow, tiger, rabbit, dragon, snake, horse, goat, monkey, chicken, dog, and pig. To thank them for coming, Buddha made each animal the master for one year and gave

DID YOU KNOW THAT . . .

. . . pet rats are descended from laboratory animals?

Brown rats were used in animal research as early as the nineteenth century. Albinos that had already been tamed were selected as lab animals. In breeding rat strains for research, the peaceable and trusting nature of the creatures was an important criterion from the outset. All rats kept as pets are descended from laboratory rats, and like them they are characterized by a special closeness to humans.

Ganesh is accompanied on his travels by a rat that serves him as a mount. Around twenty thousand rats live in the rat temple Karni Mata in northern it the power to determine every fate and every event during its reign. People who are born in the year of the rat are considered wise, cautious, and charming.

The Way Rats Live

The power of a top athlete, the nimbleness of a tightrope walker, the nose of a bloodhound: The success formula of rats is in the fact that they are not specialists, but rather use all their abilities for every challenge.

DECATHLON RATHER THAN INDIVIDUAL EVENTS A marathon runner wouldn't stand much of a chance as a shot-putter, and a high jumper is no javelin thrower. Only the decathlon contenders can perform at top levels in several types of events. Rats master these multiple disciplines perfectly: They climb and balance much like monkeys, swim long distances, sprint very well for short distances, and yet are masters of long-distance running. They jump high and far, and in all instances keep their bodies under complete control.

Anatomy and Biology

Rats are generalists. And the typical characteristic of generalists is that there is nothing typical about them—neither a special trait of physique nor exclusive sense perceptions. Take climbing, for example: House rats especially are real climbing pros. Their feet are very nimble, but not specially adapted to climbing. Suppleness: Rats can force their bodies through any crack their heads fit through—a skill that's otherwise possible only for creatures without a wide collarbone. And yet the rat has a normally developed collarbone.
Physique. In phenotype all true mice, including rats, resemble one another:

They have a medium body size, the tail is long and nearly hairless, and the front and hind legs are nearly equal in length.
Fur. As with all rodents, the coat of a rat consists of soft wool and longer, coarse guard hairs. The ears are more sparsely haired, and the soles of the feet are bare. The tail, which is often perceived as bare, is not completely hairless. With their large vibrissae (whiskers) on their snout and eyes, rats can find their way in the dark (proximity orientation); likewise the guard hairs on the sides and legs react to touch. With rats living in the wild, brown, gray, and blackish shades predominate, and the belly is always lighter in color. With rats bred in captivity, the color spectrum runs from brown and gray to cream and white.

A rat is recognizable at a glance: beady eyes, small ears, bare feet, and a long, sparsely haired tail covered with horny scales. ▶

Rats live in a world of smells.
Scents determine togetherness in the pack and
are important for orientation and reproduction.

Most breeds are bred in many patterns (see pages 24–29).

Eyes. Rats are born blind; the eyes open between the fourteenth and sixteenth day of life. The field of view encompasses nearly 360 degrees, so creatures approaching from behind and from the air (birds of prey) do not go unperceived. Visual acuity is rather low, however. The retina contains almost exclusively rods as photoreceptors. Because these are more sensitive to light than the cones that make it possible to see colors, rats, which are active in the dusk and at night, see better in the dark than humans do; however, they are nearly color-blind. Harsh light harms their eyes, especially if color pigments are not present, as with albinos (see Tip, page 18).

Nose. Rats are "nose creatures" (macrosmatic). Their extensive nasal mucous membrane is responsible for their highly developed sense of smell. Scents also play an important role in such things as communication, orientation, reproduction, and identifying enemies.

Jacobson's Organ. The scent organ under the nostrils serves in the perception of scent substances.

Teeth. The large incisors, which are for gnawing and grow continually, are typical of rodents. There is one rodent tooth in each half of each jaw. The front side has a hard, yellowish-orange colored layer on the enamel. Similarly distinctive for rodents is the large space (diastema) between the rodent teeth and the molars (three of each in each half of the jaw). There are no canine teeth or pre-molars. Rats do not lose their baby teeth. The rodent teeth erupt on the eighth to tenth day of life. To keep them short, they must continually be abraded through gnawing. Because the backs of the teeth contain no dentine (tooth enamel) and wear away much more quickly, the rodent teeth are always self-sharpening.

Ears. The ears are relatively small and sparsely covered with hair. They can be moved independently of each other.

◀ *It usually doesn't take long for rats to become comfortable around humans. Humans also get used as climbing trees. Rats show their affection by snuggling and nibbling the ear.*

Rats are born deaf; the outer ears open after two to four days.

Feet and Claws. Rats' feet are bare; the front feet have four toes with claws, and the rear feet have five. The thumbs are vestigial and have no claws.

Tail. Rats' tails are covered with horny scales that are fused into rings. Nearly body length (see chart, page 11), they are only sparsely covered with hair. The skin of the tail is characterized by a predetermined breaking point: It rips off when a rat is picked up or pulled by the tail, and makes it possible for it to get away from enemies.

Sex Organs. In adult males (bucks) the testicles are easy to see under the tail. There is a double row of teats on the stomach of the female. Female rats are recognizable by the three orifices of anus, vagina, and urethra, which are close to one another. In males the distance between the anus and the penis is relatively large.

Exceptional Qualities

Harder's Gland. This gland in the inside corner of the eye produces a reddish secretion that probably cleans and takes care of the eye.

Sweating. Rats have no sweat glands; temperature control is handled by a few less thickly haired body parts, such as the tail and the ears.

Divided Stomach. A rat's stomach is divided by a fold. This characteristic and the lack of a vomiting reflex mean that rats are incapable of vomiting to get rid of indigestible material.

Sense Perceptions

Rats are active in the dusk and at night. In addition to their sense of smell and touch, their sense of hearing is particularly well developed.

Vision. In the dusk rats can even distinguish gray tones that are very similar to one another. They can also detect movement very well, but stationary objects may often go totally undetected. Visual acuity is minimal. The fields of vision of the eyes, which are on the sides of the head, overlap in just one small area, so that rats can barely see spatially (stereoptically), and they judge distances poorly. But the position of the eyes makes it possible for them to see nearly 360 degrees without changing their head position.

Hearing. Rats can perceive even the faintest sounds and can locate them precisely by directing their outer ears like directional antennae toward the source of the noise. Their upper hearing threshold is more than 80,000 Hz in the ultrasound range that is inaudible to humans. Even communication among pack members (see page 21) takes place mostly in the ultrasound range. The high-frequency tones are produced by forcing air through a small opening in the vocal cords. The eardrum in rats is covered with fine furrows that help in transmitting these signals.

Sense of Balance. The balance organ in the inner ear is highly developed and exceptionally effective. It enables rats to balance even on the thinnest ropes and to run over small footbridges with impunity.

Smell. Rats live in a world of scents. With their more than ten million sensory cells sensitive to smells (humans have two million) they can locate sources of smells in less than fifty milliseconds. As a result, rats are among the best sniffers in the animal kingdom. In so doing, a rat smells as if through the right and the left nostril. The sense of smell helps in finding food, smelling out enemies, identifying members of the pack by the group-specific scent, and checking a partner's willingness to mate. Rats mark by depositing droplets of urine that provide other rats with information and serve as orientation aids. With their fine noses, rats can also perceive illnesses. For example, in laboratories they are used successfully for such things as testing saliva samples for tuberculosis. Even in locating for land mines the rat's nose surpasses high-tech search devices. In contrast to dogs that are trained to locate mines, rats have the advantage of being too light to set off a mine.

Touch. The whiskers and guard hairs (see page 15) react to the tiniest movements. They provide the rats with current information about their position in space and the condition of their immediate surroundings, and even make it

TIP

Protecting Red Eyes from Light

A rat's sense of sight is adapted to a life in the dusk and the night. Intense light will harm their eyes over time. This is particularly true for the red eyes of albinos, which lack pigmentation. Make sure that the cage dweller never has an opportunity to look directly into a lamp or a spotlight.

The perfect residential landscape for rats, this has lots of hiding places and neat items for sport and play.

possible for them to find their way in complete darkness and without scent markings. The whiskers do not need to come into direct contact with objects and surfaces. They also register local air currents and eddies, such as the ones that occur inside the walls of houses. The pressure-sensitive receptors in rats' feet provide information about the structure and the material of the underground area and strike an alarm even in response to the tiniest vibrations in the floor. As with other animals, it is known that rats leave their burrows and hiding places long before an earthquake.

Taste. The taste buds on the tongue provide the rat with lots of information about the ingredients and formulation of the food. As with smells, a rat evidently stores up data on the digestibility and taste of every type of food. It will not return to a food that has once been deemed inedible, and it realizes when an accustomed food has been changed (see page 75).

Orientation. The spatial relationships in the environment are stored in the rat's brain as three-dimensional maps. The "surveillance camera" in its head perceives every change, and can even go through directions and actions in reverse (spatial memory).

Structure and Activities of the Rat Pack

Rats are social animals and cannot survive without their group. Many activities are carried out by several or all members of the pack.

Can My Rats See Colors?

Rats react mainly to movements. They perceive various shades of gray, but their ability to see colors is not well developed. However, you can still see if your pets react to different colors (red, green, blue, yellow).

The Test Begins

○ You will need a run with two sides (at about a 45-degree angle), one of them colored, one white. Put a treat at the end of the colored run. Repeat several times.

○ The experiment is the same, but the colored run (with the treat) is now on the other side. Which one do the rats choose? Repeat the test with three sides in different colors. The treat is always placed on the same side. After each test, wash the run with hot water.

My Test Results:

- A pack of rats that live in the wild will be made up of at least twenty, and frequently forty to sixty, and sometimes up to two hundred animals.
- The community is generally a family clan whose members are related to one another.
- A group structure is not immediately identifiable. Single males have territories with several females. But there are also "subordinate relationships," in which several males live in association with many females.
- The pack members recognize one another by their group-specific scent. Strange animals with a different scent are attacked and driven away.
- Communication within the group takes place through a complex vocal and body language with many gestures and sounds that avoids conflicts.
- Reciprocal body grooming is among the most important social contacts, with abundant licking and nibbling of the fur.
- Rats mark all objects that they consider theirs with drops of urine. With house rats this even includes the trusted human.
- Females that are ready to reproduce can mate with several males; one male regularly belongs with several females.
- Female rats in the pack that are friends with one another commonly share in raising the young and taking care of stray young animals.

▶ Generally pack members go out together (at least in pairs) to search for food or to reconnoiter unfamiliar territory. The rats also cooperate in defending the territory.

Rat Language

Vocal Language. Rats communicate with one another principally in the ultrasound range, which is inaudible to humans. Every day they send out thousands of high-frequency messages, with which they warn other pack members of dangers, alert them to food sources and their location, and report on how they are feeling.

The following utterances are audible to humans:

▶ Hissing and snorting are sounds of threat and warning, used to ward off intruders.
▶ Peeping is the typical anxiety sound that is used, for example, by baby rats that have been left alone, to call their mother.
▶ Teeth gnashing can express both well-being and fear or excitement. Only the accompanying body language makes it clear what the rat is trying to say.

The rats' "secret language" is intended to protect them from enemies. But some of their opponents have also developed effective eavesdropping systems to listen in on the same wavelength—house cats, for instance.

Body Language. In contrast to the vocal language, many forms of expression in body language are comprehensible to humans.

▶ Greeting: mutual sniffing of muzzle and anal regions
▶ Threatening: slowed-down movements on stiff legs, body placed sideways to the other rat, fur standing on end, eyes half shut
▶ Submission: lying on side or back in posture of humility
▶ Checking things out: rat holds its nose up in the air and sniffs

Behaviors You Need to Know

▶ Cuddling: Two or more rats lie close together or even on top of one another. Regular physical contact

Important social contact: In mutual body care the rats lick and nibble one another's fur.

with other rats is vitally important. In its absence, rats become sick.

▶ Hiding: Rats feel secure in cracks and corners, and from there they observe their surroundings.

▶ Eating: Eating is done in typical sitting posture. The food is held with the forepaws.

▶ Boxing: Male rats fight to see who is the stronger. The combatants perch on their hind legs and strike one another (boxing).

▶ Care: Rats perform thorough body care. This includes washing the fur and the face, plus nibbling the toes and claws.

Scent check: Rats sniff one another on the muzzle and usually also in the anal area when they greet and get to know one another.

▼

A Little Color Science

Nowadays rat fanciers have a choice among the widest variety of fur colors and patterns—from monochrome animals to impressively patterned Huskies and Barebacks. In addition there are smooth-haired and fluffy forms.

All pet rats are descended from brown rats that were bred for laboratory purposes (see page 14). The first rats used for breeding were albino brown rats living in the wild in the early nineteenth century in England. Today there are many different rat strains used in research around the world.

Friendly and Affectionate

Only animals that were neither shy nor nippy, and that spontaneously sought nearness to people, were suitable as laboratory rats; these criteria determined laboratory breeding for many generations. All rats that are kept as pets are direct descendants of research rats and are characterized by their friendly and outgoing nature—even though there are individual differences.

Breeding Colored Rats

First of all there is the wild color. Animals that resemble wild rats in color and markings are referred to as Agouti: The brown-gray fur has a reddish gleam; and on the belly it is dirty white to silver-gray with no clear delineation. The animals always have black eyes.

In rat breeding, the various fur colors are divided into the following categories:

▸ Agouti: Every individual hair is banded, with alternating dark and light areas. This fur type of wild-colored rats comes in many variations (such as Chocolate and Blue Agouti) and all markings.
▸ Non-Agouti: All hairs are uniformly colored.

The widest variety of fur patterns can occur in every fur color.

Eye Colors: Black, and dark, ruby, and light red. Animals with eyes of different colors are designated as *odd eyed*. Albinos lack the pigment in their hair and eyes. The hairs appear white, and in the eyes the red blood vessels are visible (eye color: pink).

TIP

Avoid Breeding Rats with Defects

Diseases and defects can occur in the following breeding forms: Rex: thin fur, little protection against cold and wet; Manx: tail is lacking or is only a stump, bone structure deformed; Dumbos: excessively large ears, hard of hearing or deaf; Naked Rats: without fur, very sensitive to heat, cold, and wet.

The Most Beautiful Rats
at a Glance

◀ Albino

Pure white specimens exist in many animal species, even though they occur very rarely in the wild. The body cells in these albino animals cannot form pigment (melanin); the skin and fur are thus uniformly white, with no spots of color or markings.

Albino ▶

The fur coat of an albino rat is pure white. Because there is no pigmentation even in their eyes, albinos always have red (pink-colored) eyes. Because of the lack of pigment, the eyes are unprotected and are sensitive to harsh light (see page 18).

Husky

Rats with Husky markings are almost always born with dark coloration. The color gets lighter as time goes by.

Husky

The white forehead blaze is typical of Husky rats; it extends as far as the ears and the throat. The fur is colored on the back and on the sides. Huskies come in a wide variety of color variations, such as Gray Husky (in the photo), Cream, Blue, and Agouti Husky.

Black Berkshire ▶

The Berkshire's fur is monochrome. Only the chest, belly, and paws are of a different color. Even rats with a white belly stripe are included among the Berkshires. The markings are particularly impressive in dark-colored animals.

Black Berkshire

The ideal Berkshire rat has four white paws, a white spot on the forehead, and a white tail tip.

Hooded

With the hooded configuration, the area from the head to the shoulders is set off in a different color. There is also a prominent back stripe, and the sides and belly are white. The rats come in various colorations.

Hooded

The broad colored stripe that runs over the back from the head to the base of the tail makes the Hooded unmistakable.

Creme Self ▶

All single-colored rats with no markings or a mask of a different color are designated with the term *self*. In contrast to this, marked is the overall term for animals with markings in their fur. Nearly all colorations common to rats (see page 23) also occur in the Self. The photo shows a Cream Self.

Creamwhite Check

In Checks the colored markings are often pale and scarcely stand out from the basic fur color.

Creamwhite Check

The body of the Check is usually light in color (white, cream, ivory, beige, silver-beige, light gray). The fur shows darker-colored spots, known as points, especially on the nose, ears, feet, and tail.

Agouti ▶

The Agouti coloration comes from the original fur color of wild rats. The fur is brown-gray with a reddish sheen, and the belly is silvery. Nowadays Agouti rats are bred in many color variations and patterns.

Agouti

In all Agouti colorations (see page 23) every hair is banded, whereas the hair in non-Agoutis is of a single, uniform color.

◀ **Black-Eyed White**

At first glance the Black-Eyed White resembles the Albino rat (Pink-Eyed White). But in contrast to the Albino, the Black-Eyed has pigmentation that is also responsible for its black eyes.

▲

Black-Eyed White

This rat's fur is pure white. The coloration is not a random occurrence, but rather the product of selective breeding.

▲

Black Self

The Black Self is another of the non-Agoutis (see page 23). It is desirable to have a unified, shiny black on the entire body without white hairs or lightening. Each individual hair is completely pigmented.

▲

Black Self

The Black Self is particularly attractive with its deep black button eyes in a dark face.

Bareback ▶

A Bareback is unmistakable: The head, chest, and shoulders are colored, sometimes darkly, and form a remarkable contrast with the rest of the body in uniform white. Because of its similarity to the Hooded (see page 26), the Bareback is often also called the American Hooded. Breeding goals are a clear demarcation between the colored front of the body and the white area and a white without shading and spots. Just like the Hooded, there are also Barebacks in every fur color.

Tricolor Check

In the Tricolor Check the patches are different in color or shade—in this rat, for example, light and dark gray.

▼

Tricolor Check

As with all Checks, the spots (points) of a Tricolor are located especially on the nose, ears, paws, and tail.

How Rats
Want to Live

Cozy places for sleeping and hiding, lookout platforms, a snack
bar that's open around the clock, and all kinds of devices for climbing
and playing—these are the things that will make rats feel at home.

A Paradise for Your Rats

Even with regular sessions outside the cage, rats spend twenty or more hours a day in their cage. So the requirements are demanding: The rat cage must offer its inhabitants every possibility for an unrestricted life in the group.

DREAM HOUSE WANTED The basic equipment is a must. But the more imagination, care, and love you put into setting up the cage and choosing the accessories, the happier you will make the gang. They will thank you with trust and affection.

Much More than a Place to Sleep

The cage is the focal point of rat life, and for the rodents it is a room for living, sleeping, eating, and playing. This is where they meet for small talk, inspire one another to go on bold chases and climbing missions, cuddle together in hammocks or sleeping houses, burrow in the bedding and the digging box, or retreat into hiding places when they are not in the mood for group living.

The More the Merrier

▶ Rats need the pack. Single life inside a cage is alien to the species and contradicts every basic need of the social rodent. A rat that lives alone languishes, develops serious behavior abnormalities, and becomes ill.
▶ Start with two, or better yet three or more, animals of the same sex (see page 54). Females from the same litter get along best with one another.
▶ The larger the group, the larger the cage must be. Even for the minimal population of two animals, a small cage is taboo. For three to four animals the minimum size is 31 × 24 × 48 inches (80 × 60 × 120 cm, length × width × height); for a group of up to ten rats, 39 × 24 × 70 inches (100 × 60 × 180 cm).
▶ Even the largest cage is no substitute for daily excursions inside the house (see page 59).

The right place for feeling good: A properly set-up cage provides the inhabitants with security and gives them plenty of stimulating opportunities to keep busy.

What Else Does Your Heart Desire?

▶ **1** **Lots of Room.** The elbow room for the inhabitants can be increased significantly by building in several stories. Stairs, ladders, and ramps connect the different levels.

▶ **2** **1,000 Mysteries.** A cleverly set-up cage continually stimulates the rats to explore the dark and mysterious corners.

▶ **3** **Playground.** The basic equipment for the rat apartment includes apparatuses for play and gymnastics; they will be in constant use.

Several Stories

As descendants of brown rats, pet rats are less gifted climbers than house rats, but verticality still plays a predominant role in their life.

▶ Multilevel apartment preferred: The cage should have living areas on several floors. Shelves, boards, and layered particle boards are good materials for building additional floors. Each floor is equipped with little houses and with equipment for play and gymnastics (see page 35), and is connected to the other floors with climbing ropes, ladders, stairs, branches, and tubes.

▶ The inhabitants reach the next floor through caps (diameter 3–4 inches/ 8–10 cm) in the usual boards. Openings for climbing through should also be provided in the mesh for the cage.

▶ Do not use any mesh for the floors. Rats cannot run properly on it and will develop foot problems (see Bumblefoot, page 89).

▶ The height of the floors is adjusted in accordance with the largest cage inhabitants. Every rat must be able to sit up on its haunches without hitting the ceiling.

▶ With very high cages, pass-through floors are an advantage, because they prevent falls from fairly significant heights. Hammocks and nets also provide protection (see page 39).

▶ Rabbit and guinea pig cages are not suitable for rats: They have a large surface area, but they are too low and can't be divided into several floors.

Custom-Tailored Cage Bars

▶ The bars for a rat cage run horizontally so they can be used as climbing aids.

▶ The size of the mesh must be such that the rodents can neither get out nor get their head stuck. In a cage with adult animals, the mesh should be about ½ to ⅝ inch (12–15 mm); for young rats up to the twelfth week of life, no more than 5⁄16 inch (10 mm).

▸ To avoid having to construct special accommodations for baby rats, attach small animal screen on the inside of the cage mesh. It can be removed once the young rats are grown up.

▸ It is easier to observe the rats in cages with dark mesh than in models with galvanized or shiny mesh.

Doors and Hatches

If the daily cage duties are set up to be toilsome and time-consuming, they often are performed only perfunctorily. To keep this from happening, all areas of the cage must be accessible through large doors and hatches. With factory-made cages, it often makes sense to build in additional doors to make it easy to remove leftover food and droppings completely, remove the accessories for cleaning, or put the inhabitants into another cage without getting them upset. But be careful: Doors are the weak spots in rodent homes. The clever residents are quick to figure out where a door doesn't close properly or a lock jams.

A Basin for Cleanliness

A bottom pan made of solid plastic 6 to 8 inches (15–20 cm) high prevents the little diggers from spreading the bedding all through the surroundings as they burrow.

TIP

Emergency Repairs

You can guess who will be the first to figure out if somewhere in the cage is a crack large enough for a nimble rodent to fit through, or if a door does not close properly. Time is of the essence: Repair it as quickly as possible, because otherwise your rats will keep trying to break out.

The Right Location for the Rat Cage

One important criterion that must be addressed in purchasing a cage is the issue of the proper location. Generally the right cage size represents a compromise between the requirements of the future inhabitants and the limitations in their living space.

cycle, twelve hours of light followed by twelve hours of darkness.

Villa with a View. The rat cage does not belong on the floor. The fear of enemies from the air (birds of prey) is deep in rats, and a person reaching into the cage from above will quickly put them into a panic. The best choice is a place about 40 to 48 inches (100–120 cm) high. This also makes it easier to clean the cage.

A Super Climate. The room temperature should be between 70 and 75°F (21 and 24°C), with a humidity of 50–60

DID YOU KNOW THAT . . .

. . . rats recognize you mainly by smell?

Rats are not as blind as bats, but they are a little nearsighted. This is not a huge problem for animals that are active in the dusk. A good nose that doesn't miss a scent is more important. Even people are recognized primarily by scent. Misunderstandings can be avoided if you wear a shirt that smells of rat when you deal with your animals. The "rat shirt" immediately notifies the crew in the cage that their best friend is coming.

In the Center of Things. Rats are full of impetuosity, and there is always something going on in the pack. Still, the rodents are curious about everything that goes on around them on their home turf. Thus, the cage should not be relegated to a remote corner or room that doesn't get much use. In addition, constant closeness to people encourages trust and builds confidence more quickly in newly arrived rats.

A Twelve-Hour Day. Where the cage is located, the rhythm of light and dark should alternate for an equal day–night

percent. The rat cage must not stand on a heater or in direct sunlight.

Keep the Noise Down. Rats have very good but sensitive ears. They usually get used to normal noises in the surroundings quickly, but they are visibly afraid of excessive and pervasive noise. So don't put the cage near the TV or the stereo.

Protection from Draft. Respiratory infections are among the most common illnesses in rats. In many cases the cold is caused by a draft. Make sure the cage is protected from drafts.

The worst thing for rats is feeling sad inside their cage. An **anti-boredom package** with lots of opportunities for playing, climbing, and hiding will keep your gang happy.

Seting Up the Cage

Rats need to keep busy. They want to climb, dig, balance, and go on tours of discovery. They need eating places and toilet areas, sleeping houses, places to cuddle, observation platforms, and hiding places. A cleverly and lovingly set-up cage will be a stimulating adventure land for the inhabitants and will provide them with surprises even after weeks. And if all the corners ever get explored, the rat aficionado can certainly give them a stimulating new toy that will keep the rodent gang occupied for a long time.

A Climbing Tree

A strong, forked branch that reaches nearly to the roof of the cage makes a perfect climbing tree. Because the wood will also get gnawed, you should never use branches, twigs, or roots of unknown origin. Before putting the branch into the cage, scrub it thoroughly with hot water. To make it easier for older rats to climb up it, you can wrap it in sisal or coconut rope. Connecting ropes create a connection between the side branches, and platforms and houses in the forks of the branch serve as lookout points and sleeping places. Important point: The climbing tree needs a solid stand on the bottom of the cage. In addition it must be securely anchored to the cage bars in several places.

Floorboards

Layered particle board, laminated or waterproof, and wood varnished with a nontoxic finish (wood finish according to toy safety standards as identified in DIN EN 71) and plastic boards are the best materials for building additional floors. But boards with a glued-on veneer must often be exchanged for different ones, because the veneer will get gnawed. Not only the running surfaces, but also the edges should be protected from moisture and urine, for example with waterproof glue or varnish. In a wire mesh cage, it is easiest to secure the boards with screws so they can be hung in place; glue or nails can be used on wood walls. In this case you can also place them on forms and angle braces—

Once the ice is broken, the rat will even take treats from the hand.

*Most rats think swings are neat. All they
need is someone to push.*

houses for guinea pigs. If you build a
house yourself, wood is the right material to use. As with the floorboards, it
must be protected against urine and
dampness. One idea is an overturned
clay flowerpot with an opening broken
into the edge. Even sturdy cardboard
will work, but it absorbs moisture and
quickly gets dirty. Hanging the houses
from the cage bars saves space. With all
models, the entrance holes must be
large enough, and there must be room
inside for two or three animals. Houses
with a flat roof offer an additional
observation deck. Good nesting materials include newspaper, tissues, paper
towels, toilet paper, and many similar
materials. The stuffing must be replaced
regularly. Cotton (including fluff for
hamsters) is dangerous: It can get
wrapped around paws and toes and cut
off circulation so that their digits wither
and die.

Water Bottles

A water bottle with a ball valve attached
to the outside of the cage wire is the
only correct, hygienic, and irreproach-
able drinking device for rats. At least
two water bottles are part of the basic
cage equipment. Open water dishes
pose a health risk, because dirt and disease pathogens can accumulate in them.

Food Dishes

When rats eat, they like to sit on the
edge of the food dish. To keep it from
tipping over, you need to select a very
stable model, such as a ceramic one.
Serve grains and succulent foods in separate bowls. Fairly large groups need
several food dishes. Don't place them
next to the cage wire, but rather in the
center of the cage. Because the pack's

that way everything can be taken out
easily for cleaning.

Bedding

The bedding for the cage must neutral-
ize odors, be absorbent, soft, and dust-
free, and have no particular scent. Good
choices include sawdust, wood pellets,
litter, and straw made from hemp or
cornhusks. You should avoid using sand,
peat, and clay kitty litter. The depth of
the bedding layer should be around 4
inches (10 cm).

House

Houses are essential components in a
rat cage. Even if several residents often
sleep together in one house, there
should be accommodations on every
floor so that one animal can withdraw
at will. Pet shops offer only a few houses
for rats, and it's best to steer clear of

The Basic Equipment
at a Glance

◀ Climbing Branch and Litter

A large branch or climbing tree is the focal point of rat life. It's an invitation for exercise and climbing, and it offers the best outlook point (far left). Rats can dig to their heart's content in the loose bedding (photo left).

Houses and Toilet ▶

Little houses for sleeping and relaxing should be on every floor of the cage (right). Rats get used to a small animal toilet when it is set up in their preferred "business corner" (photo far right).

◀ Food Dish and Water Bottles

The food dish must be stable and heavy enough so it doesn't tip over if a rat perches on the edge (far left photo). A water bottle with a ball valve is a neat thing and the only proper water dispenser for the rodents (left).

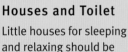

frequently used "runways" follow the cage wire, any food along the cage edge quickly gets dirty.

Climbing Ropes and Rope Ladders

Climbing ropes and rope ladders make bored rats lively. With the ropes and ladders they can directly reach exposed areas such as the outer branches of the climbing tree or individual outlook platforms. Climbing ropes made of hemp, sisal, or coconut fibers are especially durable and offer the claws a secure grip. Thick knots in the rope are used as lookouts and make it easier for less nimble old-timers to climb. Cross ropes can be used to connect to perches and branches, or can be strung through the whole cage. They encourage and develop the sense of balance and obviously are lots of fun for the effervescent rodents.

Stairs and Ramps

In addition to the climbing tree, stairs and ramps form the main connection between the various floors. Hard plastic is easier than wood to keep clean, but it doesn't provide much traction for rodent feet, so plastic ramps should be used only at a low angle. On steep staircases, railings keep the users from slipping off the side or falling down.

Swing

Rats are madly in love with everything that moves and can be moved. A swing is one of the clear favorites among toys.

MY PET

How Fit Are My Rats?

"Full speed ahead" is the motto for most rats when it comes to games and sports. But the individual differences are large, and the older rats usually take things easier. This test will show who has an advantage in fitness.

The Test Begins:
- ○ Who is the best climber in the group and climbs the rope in record time?
- ○ Which animals prefer to take the stairs to get to the upper levels?
- ○ Do the rats prefer climbing ropes with knots where they can take a rest?
- ○ Who is the best at balancing on the planks and cross ropes?
- ○ Is the swing in constant motion because it's so much fun for the whole troupe?

My Test Results:

A nifty tower: A climbing garden with ramps, ropes, platforms, and houses provides lots of excitement. When the rats are running around free, this keeps the lively bunch always within view and keeps the saucy explorers from straying too far.

You usually can avoid arguments over who gets to use the swing by putting in a second one.

Tubes and Tunnels

Wild brown rats live in underground burrows and in hiding places close to the ground. Their pet relatives are also magically attracted to mysterious cracks and dark holes. Tunnels and tubes must therefore be part of every cage. Hamster tunnels are not appropriate: They are too narrow, and the rodent feet have no traction on the smooth surfaces.

Hammocks

A hammock is ideal for relaxing, as another sleeping place, and as an observation platform. Choose a strong, preferably dirt-resistant material such as denim or a cleaning rag. Careful: Towel material consists of curled thread, and the rat's claws and teeth can become caught in the loops.

Hammocks have another function: As safety nets under cross ropes and runways they can prevent falls onto the bottom of the cage.

Digging Box and Food for Nibbling

▸ Rats are passionate diggers. They burrow in the bedding, but a digging box is even more fun. They can be filled alternately with paper, sand, or leaves and thus remain interesting—especially if it rustles mysteriously or some treats are hidden inside. A digging box placed in the room while the rats are out free will keep them in view.

▸ Rats need material to gnaw on to keep the rodent teeth short. Good choices include branches that have not been sprayed, chew stones made from pumice, untreated wood, and even dog biscuits.

A Toilet Dish

Rats usually deposit their droppings in a specific corner of the cage. If you install a toilet here (a small animal toilet or a plastic bowl), it will quickly gain acceptance. Appropriate filler materials include bird sand from a pet shop, and newspaper.

Everything for Fitness

Climbing is in a rat's blood. But since every animal is a little personality with its own preferences, there are all kinds

Rats are natural-born
tightrope walkers.

of climbers. In order to meet all requirements, the cage should be outfitted with as many different types of climbing devices as possible.

Climbing Rope. The climbing rope is the quickest way to go up, but the ascent requires nimbleness and strength. The rope must therefore provide adequate hold for the claws, and must be thick enough for "oncoming traffic" to get by. Generally the rope is attached top and bottom; a free-hanging rope must be reachable when the animals sit up on their haunches. A platform on the top side makes it easier to get off.

Rope Ladders. A rope ladder is not a substitute for a climbing rope. Climbing it is laborious, especially for older animals, and sometimes they are left hanging on the rungs. A rope ladder is easiest to master when it is secured top and bottom and stretched tight.

Tightrope. All items inside the cage can be connected with side ropes. They pose a particular challenge to the inhabitants in continually testing their sense

of balance. Once a tightrope walker negotiates the rope in one direction, a test run in the other direction is soon to follow. Despite their well-developed sense of balance and a tail that can be used as a safety rope in an emergency, rats are not immune to falls. To keep a false step from ending up badly, you should stretch a hammock or a net under every rope.

Stairs and Ramps. There are stairs in every tidy house with several floors (see page 38). The older residents in the rat cage are happy to pass up the strenuous climbing rope, and a rat that is carrying food or a toy will also prefer the stairs. Ramps take up more room than stairs. Cross strips on very steep ramps provide the needed grip.

Tubes. At an incline of 20 to 30 degrees, the only choices are tubes made of materials that provide some traction, such as drainage pipes, clay pipes, and strong cardboard tubes. In plastic tubes the rats will slip back as they try to climb up. Fairly long tubes should be provided with several exit holes.

Cage Bars. The cage bars are a universal climbing device: Horizontal bars are the best choice. Be sure to get a sturdy metal wire with the correct mesh size (see page 32). Plastic-coated bars are not a good choice because they will get gnawed. The larger the free climbing surface, the better.

Pants and Pockets. A cut-off pants leg (linen, denim) or a jute bag can be used to make neat climbing tubes. Attach the pants leg or the bag to a floorboard; the rats will climb in and out of it. And the front or seat pockets are likewise great hiding places.

The Best Climbing Devices
at a Glance

Free climbing ▶

Balancing on a slack rope requires a lot of skill and physical control (right). Climbing the cage bars is child's play for this trio of mountaineers (far right).

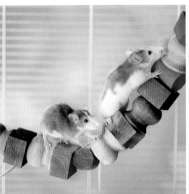

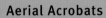

◀ A Climb and a View

The house roof is a perfect place for resting and taking in the sights (far right photo). A branch or a stair serves as a climbing aid so that the rats can get back into the cage by themselves after running around free (left).

Aerial Acrobats ▶

Professional climbers like rats don't shy away from daring actions—even if getting off the swing poses problems (right) or the rope ladder unexpectedly tips to the side (far right photo).

A Ready-Made or a Homemade Cage?

If you don't feel up to making a cage for your rats, you can locate a ready-made one at a pet shop or on the Internet. Whether you buy one or build one yourself, you should keep a few important points in mind.

A Ready-Made Cage. Unfortunately there are a limited number of cages available that will meet all living conditions for rats—both in pet shops and on the Internet.

▸ A rat cage must be at least 3 feet (1 m) high, and even significantly higher if there are more than four inhabitants. Most of the cages available for sale are too low, even the ones that are sold specifically as rat cages.

▸ Cages for guinea pigs and hamsters are too low, and therefore don't provide the rodents with sufficient climbing opportunities.

▸ Large bird cages generally are high enough, but they are not escape-proof because of the excessively large gaps in the bars, and doors that don't latch securely.

▸ Aquariums and terrariums are out of the question. They provide inadequate ventilation, additional floors cannot be installed, and it is impossible for the rats to climb in these tanks.

▸ Large rodent cages and chipmunk cages come fairly close to providing the desired accommodations for rats with respect to dimensions and wire mesh. But even in this case the owner must invest lots of care and imagination in setting up the cage so that it is rat-proof. This is particularly true for fairly large groups.

A Homemade Cage. A homemade cage has several advantages: It meets the expectations of the builder with respect to size and appearance; it can be adapted to the number and the preferences of the inhabitants, as well as to the conditions of the living space; and it can be constructed from inexpensive materials that are available everywhere and easy to work with.

▸ If you want to build your rat cage from the first board to the last screw, you will find everything you need in a hardware store: lumber, particle board, angle irons, bolts, wire, and plastic strips (to go around the base of the cage).

▸ Wire mesh (small animal wire) is sold in rolls in hardware stores. With a

◂ *A homemade rat cage: A little manual skill and some supplies from the hardware store is all it takes to make a cage that will meet your needs.*

mesh size of a little more than ¼ inch (10 × 10 mm) it will be easy for the animals to climb on it. Make sure the wire has no sharp edges.

▶ You can build a cage even if you are not skilled with your hands, by covering only the front of the cage in wire and making the other sides of wood. It is easy to attach boards for additional stories and accessories to the walls.

▶ You can find appropriate bottom pans made of solid plastic in department stores and hardware stores. The rim must be at least 6 inches (15 cm) high.

▶ If you don't have the time or the patience to make a cage yourself, you can turn necessity into a virtue and remodel an old cabinet into a rat home: All you have to do is remove the cabinet doors and stretch small-animal wire across the front.

▶ Boards must be finished with non-toxic varnish (see page 35) or covered with foil. Don't forget to protect the edges from rat urine. The most important thing is for all the pieces to fit together tightly to thwart escapes. This applies to the corners of the cage, and particularly to the doors and hatches and all locations that are fashioned from different materials.

Keep It Practical

Whether you buy or build, make sure that the cage is easy to get into so that there is no difficulty working inside it. Doors and hatches must open wide enough, and must be made so that you can reach every floor and corner in the cage without strain. That is the only way you can keep the rodent home clean in the long run and replace individual items as needed.

CHECKLIST

Rat Cage Technical Requirements

The daily program inside the rat cage includes wild climbing parties and chases, daring leaps, and tightrope action. To keep the animals from getting hurt, everything must be built solidly and attached securely.

○ Choose a cage with bars that run horizontally and a mesh size of no greater than about a ½ inch (1 cm).

○ With young rats the mesh size must not exceed about $5/16$ inch (10 mm). Alternatively, you can put small-animal wire on the inside of the bars.

○ All doors and hatches must be solid and escape-proof. You may need to provide them with a latch or a padlock.

○ Large front doors (one- or two-panel) make it easier to set up and clean the cage.

○ When you set up the cage, make sure that everything is securely attached. Regularly check mountings and connections.

○ The inside diameter of tubes and tunnels must be large enough that the fattest rat can go through without getting stuck.

○ Large openings make it easier to climb up to the next floor.

○ Nets and hammocks prevent falls.

○ Railings make ramps and steps secure.

The Exciting World of Rats

It doesn't take much to kindle enthusiasm for animals in most children. But to keep a four-legged comrade from turning into a plaything, you need to explain all about animals to your children. This applies especially to small pets such as rats.

CHILDREN ARE CURIOUS and have a craving for knowledge. They are wide-eyed over anything that has to do with animals, especially when the object of their attention lives under the same roof, so no further stimulus is needed in getting them to understand the animals' requirements and behavior.

The Example of the Parents

Rats are fascinating. For children this statement applies without reservation: In contrast to many adults, when they see a rat, they feel neither fear nor revulsion. This distance becomes part of them only when they continually witness defensive reactions in their parents and other people in their immediate vicinity. Children whose parents are attentive and caring with rats, on the other hand, develop an unbiased and affectionate relationship with the rodents that will survive the passage of time.

As Adventurous as a Fairy Tale

Animal life can be exciting, and a rat's life is particularly so. Even children three and four years old can be captivated by stories about rats and their special qualities. Take the time to tell them about the extraordinary sense perceptions, the intelligence, the complex language, the hidden life, and the peaceful society of the pack. It certainly is not out of the question for the rat stories to supersede the nightly classic fairy tales.

First Acquaintances

Young children up to the age of seven should not be left alone with the rats. At this age, getting to know the rats mainly involves continually observing them and their typical behavior, and peppering the adults with questions when something is going on in the cage that they don't understand. This works best when the children and adults regularly sit in front of the rat cage for a half hour and share their observations. This is guaranteed to offer as much variety as children's programming on television.

Gentle Contact

The little ones can carefully touch and stroke a rat in the parent's hand. In so doing they feel the soft body and move the delicate legs and feet. But small children are still not ready to pick up and hold a rat by themselves.

Professional Help. Experienced owners will gladly give advice to beginners who want to make their own cage. You can make contacts through rat clubs and on Internet sites devoted to pet rats (see the addresses on page 141).

A Deluxe Rat Cage

On Internet sites for animal accessories and in well-stocked pet shops you can find a small selection of good-quality cages that are also appropriate for rats.

▸ Example 1: Cage with aluminum frame, outside dimensions 33 × 22 × 58 inches (85 × 55 × 147 cm), two large 13 × 11 inch (34 × 28 cm) front doors, black bars of .078 inch (2 mm) wire, mesh size ¼ inch (6 mm). Four rollers with locks, removable bottom grate for easier cleaning of bottom pan. Wooden floors, ladders, and houses. Six-inch (16 cm) plastic skirts keep bedding from getting scattered around the room when the rats dig. Price: approximately $250.

▸ Example 2: Rodent cage made of powder-coated metal with roller, dimensions 47 × 32 × 79 inches (120 × 81 × 201 cm), two main doors 16 × 12 inches (40 × 31 cm), mesh size ½ inch (1 cm). Five metal ladders, three metal bowls, four double dishes. Price: approximately $375.

Even these and similar cages must be adapted to the rats' special needs—for example with additional floors, houses, and climbing opportunities.

1 **Living in Style.** There is no upper limit to the size of the cage. By adding additional floors the living space can be multiplied several times with the same outside dimensions.

2 **Open Door Day.** Even rats that live in a large rodent villa need a chance to run around inside the house every day. During this time the cage door is kept open so that the parolees can go back inside at any time.

Questions About
Cages and Equipment

I don't feel like building a cage for the rats. How much does a ready-made cage for three or four animals cost?

The larger the cage, the more variety you can build in when you set it up. So there is also (practically) no upper limit for the price. For around $200 you can get a solid cage with dimensions of 31 × 24 × 47 inches (80 × 60 × 120 cm) (length × width × height) that will work for a group of rats. But usually the equipment for most commercially made cages is not ideal, so when you set one up, oftentimes you still must work on it and install additional floors.

I am remodeling a small cabinet into a cage. The front is small-animal wire. How do I make the doors?

One large door that takes up half the front, or even better, the whole front, is ideal. It should be held in a secure metal frame and extend to the lower edge of the cage. This will make it easier for your rats to get out on their daily free run. To keep from having to open the large door every time you reach in, build in two smaller doorways. With a main door that takes up a whole side both of these are located in the large door, and in addition there is a hatch next to them. Measure in advance to determine the best location for the additional entrance to the cage.

Newspaper is soft and very absorbent. But will it hurt the rats if they eat it?

Formerly newspaper was not harmless because of the printer's ink. But with today's printing processes there is no longer any danger if the rodents nibble on it. The situation is different with paper that was printed with laser or inkjet printers. Under no circumstances should this be put into the cage.

Soon two new rats will be joining the three that are already in my cage. Then things will be crowded. I have heard of expandable cages. How do they work?

Expandable cages are based on a building block system: Every module is constructed so that it can easily be added as needed to other building blocks in a composite system. Usually there are a basic module and expansion modules, all with the same dimensions. Unfortunately, this type of expandable cage system is rarely sold in pet shops. If you simply want to offer your rats a little more elbow room, you can, for example, put in some additional houses attached right to the cage bars rather than on an existing floor, or some that hang down like a light from one of the floors.

? **My rats are extremely curious and continually inspect every corner in the cage. Will their urge to discover be satisfied if I frequently rearrange the equipment in the cage?**

Unfortunately not. It is important for the rodents to know their way around every detail and to know the precise location of all objects in the cage, the center of their territory. They can dash securely through their surroundings as though with their eyes closed only because they have internalized the topography so well. If everything suddenly changes and the houses, stairs, ladders, and climbing ropes are no longer in the accustomed locations, they can easily make a false step and take a fall. In addition, the whole troupe will feel insecure, with the result that the whole setup will be marked intensively. So always limit the renovation or exchange of items to just a few objects.

? **I am eleven years old and I think rats are neat. Unfortunately my mother won't allow any in the house because she thinks that everything will smell of rat. Is this true?**

The fear is totally ungrounded. Rats are among the cleanest of all animals, and they regularly clean themselves thoroughly. In comparison, mouse odors are much stronger. At the most, there may be a mild scent from the males when they mark. But even with this you practically have to put your nose into it. Generally speaking, odors from rat ownership occur only when cage cleaning has been neglected.

? **Is it true that cat litter can be used for the rat toilet?**

Cat litter absorbs odors and is absorbent. Thus, it is also appropriate for rats. But there are two limitations: You should not give your rats clay litter. The particles are hard and sharp, and this is not good for sensitive rodent paws. In addition, there are almost always chemical additives in clay litter. These problems are not present in softwood bedding. In no case should you use cat litter that clumps up when it gets wet. What's good in the case of cats and facilitates cleaning can end badly with rats: The animals may eat the lumps, and they may clump together in their stomach.

? **Our cage is on rollers. Should we put it outdoors so that the rats can get some fresh air?**

Rats frequently suffer from respiratory problems. The main cause is draft. They are not immune to this even in the corner of the terrace. So it's best to leave the cage inside the house. If the front is covered with wire, there is no accumulation of odors, and there is adequate fresh air.

Acquaintance and Acclimation

Rats are careful but curious creatures. It usually doesn't take long for the new cage dwellers to make friends with their owner and the new surroundings.

The Right Start
in Rat Life

Rats are small animals, and they spend most of the day inside their cage. Still, they pose demands that every owner must understand before making a purchase. Here's how to avoid problems from the outset.

RESPONSIBILITY FOR LITTLE CUDDLERS
Rats need the company of other rats: They feel safe and secure only in the society of the pack. But humans are just as important: Pet rats need and seek out closeness and physical contact with their owners—regardless of whether they are kept in a pair or a group of ten. For rat owners this trust is the best proof that they have a knack for dealing with their rodents (see page 53). They also need to do justice to the creatures' requirements.

What You Need to Consider Before Buying a Rat

Rats are clever and charming. But people who yield to their feelings and spontaneously decide to own rats are doing no good to themselves or to the animals. Before making a purchase you should objectively consider the following points.

Allergy Test. Today more than ever before people experience allergic reactions. Like other furry animals, rats can trigger allergies. If in doubt, an allergy test from a skin doctor will provide clarification.

A Joint Consideration. As a single person you don't have to consider other people. But otherwise, in the case of a life partner, children, grandmother, or shared apartment, everyone must be in agreement about owning a rat. Many people are repelled by rats or are afraid of them—even if the cage is located in a different room and they never come into direct contact with the animals.

Space Considerations. The larger the better: A rat cage requires a lot of space and must not be relegated to a corner or a room that is rarely used. Can a cage be integrated into your living space?

Animal Life. When rats live under the same roof with other animals, problems may occur. The rodents are prey animals

Cuddle time: ▶
Children are captivated by the lively, trusting rodents. And for the rats there is nothing better than cuddling with their trusted playmate.

for dogs and cats, and despite numerous examples of a peaceful coexistence, the harmony can quickly turn to danger. In addition, rats pose a potential danger to smaller pets, which rats may fight with and injure.

Free Exercise. The daily free time outside the cage is a must for the entire rodent band. Around two hours is best; with larger groups, the creatures don't all get their excursion at the same time. Can you afford the time for this? Can you deal with the fact that they will mark here and there, and that a rat may vanish behind a bookcase sometimes?

Cuddle Time. Rats need lots of attention and physical contact with people. The regular cuddle times in the morning or evening solidify trust. Will this fit into your daily routine?

Care. Before buying a rat, you must be certain who is responsible for care, feeding, and cleaning the cage, and who can step in as a replacement.

Financial Planning. Owning small pets doesn't make a huge hole in the pocketbook. But you should not cut corners with the cage and equipment. There could be additional costs for medical attention and for care for the pets during vacations.

Children and Rats. Nearly all children are excited by rats. It is the parents' responsibility to tone down somewhat the often exuberant attention, and to guide the children to thoughtful, careful dealings with the animals (see page 56). This takes time and patience.

Medicine Man. Before buying a rat, establish contact with a veterinarian practicing in the vicinity who has experience in treating small mammals. The veterinarian can give you important tips for the first weeks with the rodents, and may know the addresses of competent animal sitters.

Contraceptive Measures. Rats are exceptionally prolific creatures. For reliable prevention of offspring, it's best to keep the sexes segregated. In a mixed group the males must be neutered. People who want to breed rats are the only ones who should keep females in the same cage with unneutered males.

Finding Homes for the Offspring. In no case should you undertake breeding rats until you have identified reliable recipients for the young animals.

Rat Sitters. It is not always quick and easy to find a reliable vacation replacement to take care of the rats. Begin your search shortly after buying the animals and brief the caregiver (see Animal Sitter's Guidelines, pages 136–137).

TIP

Stress-Free Transport

Like all small pets, rats should travel only in an escape-proof box. The transport box must be well ventilated, and preferably lined with familiar bedding. A house will provide security and a place for retreat. Food should be provided only on fairly long trips.

Where Do I Get My Rats?

Pipes, tunnels, and dark caves have a magical attraction for all rats and should be present in every cage.

Regardless of the supplier you choose, none of these "reasons" should induce you to make the purchase:

▸ You feel sorry for the animals because they face an uncertain future.

▸ Friends, relatives, and acquaintances don't know where they can find homes for the offspring of their rats.

▸ At the outset you met a rat and fell head over heels for its charm and lovable nature.

▸ To keep the peace you caved in to pressure from your children.

In every case the initial prospect for a happy situation involving human and rats is very unfavorable. And it often happens that the animals are given away after only a short time.

Breeders. With animals from recognized breeders, you can generally be certain that they are healthy and free of behavior abnormalities. Still, you should take a close look at the living conditions at the breeders recommended by your veterinarian, rat clubs, and other rat owners (see page 53). Visit two or three breeders so you can compare. Even people who want a particular color variant must not avoid visiting the breeder. It is especially worthwhile for beginners to visit a show or a small-mammal fair before making a decision. There you can almost always examine animals with the appropriate color or markings.

Private Parties. Rats from private individuals are advertised primarily in the classified ad section of daily newspapers, in animal magazines, and on bulletin boards at veterinarians' offices. These often are owners who devote lots of care to their animals, but who unexpectedly have to give up the hobby because of illness or family reasons. Even though taking over such an animal seems straightforward, you should never make an impulse purchase. Take time to get to know the rats and their surroundings, and consider all the points that are important in a breeder (see facing page).

Circle of Friends. From friends and relatives who want to give up some rats for adoption you usually have a clear idea of how they keep the animals. This simplifies the decision to purchase. But at the same time there is the danger of agreeing to the deal halfheartedly or against your best judgment because you don't want to say no, or you want to do your friend a favor.

Pet Shop. A common misconception is that all pet shop animals are sourced from quantity breeders, not quality breeders. Arguments put forth are that the purchase amounts to abetting any improper accommodations and the resulting diseases and behavior prob-

lems, and that the dealers are not forced to mend their ways. Here too there certainly are some black sheep. Most of the pet shops satisfy the most important living conditions, though, as encouraged by various associations that prescribe animal welfare (see the addresses on page 141). This is also in their own interest—after all, clients in this area are much more sensitive about this than ever before. A pet shop is thus the first place most beginners and first-time buyers go to.

Animal Shelter. There are many rats in animal shelters that are waiting for a new home. There are many reasons for giving up the animals: The demands posed by the rodents are greater than expected, initial enthusiasm has turned to indifference, undesired reproduction has occurred, or there is no time to care for them. But no matter how great the rats' needs are, it still applies in an animal shelter: Don't make a hasty purchase, but rather observe the animals over several visits. And since the sexes are not always segregated, you should not rule out the possibility that you will get a pregnant female.

◄ *These three young rats still look a little fearful in the new world. But soon their curiosity will take over, and they will explore all the corners of the new home territory together.*

Your Ideal Breeder

Does the breeder meet all the following criteria? Then you can be certain of obtaining vital, affectionate animals.

▸ Lots of room: The cages should be larger than the minimum requirements specified by various animal welfare organizations (see facing page).

▸ Family ties: The cages are located where the family spends most of the day, and not in some distant room, or as often happens with rabbits, in a shed or a wing.

▸ Healthy, lively, and curious: All cage residents appear to be alert and lively. They at first remain reserved with strangers but don't hide from them. Once their curiosity wins out, they also approach the cage bars to look at you.

▸ No boredom: The rat homes are set up carefully and knowledgeably. They provide the animals with plenty of hiding places, ways to keep busy, and climbing opportunities.

▸ Clean: Leftover food and droppings are carefully removed, the bedding is loose and clean, the toilet dish is not visibly dirty. There is also practically no odor detectable near the cage.

▸ Everything fresh: Grains and food for gnawing are always available. Drinking water, fruit, and other succulent foods are provided fresh every day.

▸ Outside the cage: All rats get a chance to run around free every day.

▸ A heart and soul: The animals gladly let the owner pick them up, and cuddle on the owner's shoulder.

TEST

Do I Have a Knack for Owning a Rat?

Rats change the daily routine: They need lots of attention and regular care. Are you ready for this?

	Yes	No
1. I do things with my rat several times a day.	○	○
2. I invest patience and time to win their trust.	○	○
3. It's OK with me if they continually turn me into a climbing tree.	○	○
4. It's OK that the cage occupies a prominent place in the house.	○	○
5. Every day I let the band of little rascals run free in the house, even if they sometimes mark the furniture.	○	○
6. I am not upset to have to occasionally look for a fugitive hiding under a cupboard.	○	○
7. Cleaning the cage is something that I see as part of the caregiving program.	○	○
8. I never forget to feed the rats, and I give them fresh drinking water every day.	○	○
9. The rats are well taken care of when I'm away.	○	○
10. I always have a sharp eye peeled for the behavior of my rats and immediately notice if an animal is ailing.	○	○

TEN YESES: You are the most conscientious owner that the rats could hope for. Eight to nine yeses: The animals will be comfortable with you. Maybe you should show a little more patience and tolerance. Fewer than eight yeses: Rats are too demanding for you.

Who Finds Places for Rats?

Various rat associations and forums (see the addresses on page 141) perform emergency placement services for rats in need. Animals from excessively high animal shelter populations and impoundings are input into the placement data banks and emergency lists, along with handicapped, abused, and sick rats. You can get detailed information at the website of the appropriate hobbyist associations. Sometimes you can also report emergencies by e-mail on these sites.

How Many and What Types Should I Start With?

You have made the decision to get rats. Now the issue is how to get started in rat life: with one animal or several, a female or a male, with young animals or adults.

A sturdy, well-ventilated, and secure transparent container is a good choice for transporting a rat.

▼

Rats Need Other Rats

Never keep rats singly. Even though there is a strong relationship of trust between rat and human, that is no substitute for other rats. Animals that live alone languish. So begin with at least a pair, or better, with three or four rats. To prevent reproduction, the animals should be of the same sex.

Males or Females?

▸ Female rats remain smaller and lighter than males. Their ability to learn and their curiosity are remarkable. Usually females are also particularly agile and fond of climbing.
▸ Male rats approach everything peacefully, but are very cuddly. They have a slightly stronger odor than females.
  Individual differences are great, so thoroughly inspect your chosen animals before you buy.

Differences Between the Sexes

▸ Females: The anal, sex, and urinary orifices are located close to one another. There are two rows of teats on the belly.
▸ Males: There is a larger distance between anus and penis. In adult rats the testicles are clearly visible beneath the tail.

Young or Adult Rats?

▸ Young animals: Before reaching sexual maturity males and females are segregated. You can buy young rats starting at the weaning age of five to six weeks.
▸ With adult animals you should investigate their background, and with shelter rats this is not always possible. Rats live to be two to three years old.

HOW TO TELL IF A RAT IS HEALTHY BEFORE YOU BUY

PHYSICAL TRAITS

Fur	With a healthy animal the fur lies smoothly on the body, is free of scabs and wounds, and has no thin or bald spots.
Eyes	The eyes are clear and shiny. Discharges and incrustations are signs that the rat doesn't feel well or is sick.
Nose	The nose is clean and free from discharge and secretions. The rat does not sneeze; it breathes freely and without audible breathing noises.
Ears	Rat ears are sensitive. Scaly ears can be an indication of parasites and unclean living conditions, and injuries and tears, of trouble in the pack.
Anus	A matted anal region is an alarm signal and usually the consequence of diarrhea, which can last a long time in rats.
Paws	The tender paws can suffer on the wrong type of ground, which can produce cracking and inflammation. The claws must not be too long.
Movement	Healthy animals run and climb with no restrictions in motion, and can maintain their balance even on thin ropes.
Posture	Rats sit in a hunched position; however, an excessively arched back often indicates illness.

BEHAVIOR

Mobility	Rats love to move around. An animal that cowers in a corner is almost always ill or is subordinate to the other rats.
Eating Behavior	Healthy rats have a healthy appetite. They go to the food dish frequently, but take only small tidbits. Refusal to eat is a symptom of illness.
Curiosity	Curiosity and fondness of contact are typical of rats. Only fearful or neglected animals keep a distance from humans.

Friendship and Responsibility

Rats are wonderful playmates for children. But in their enthusiasm sometimes the children forget that the rodents pose special demands and react differently than they do. With careful guidance they quickly learn how to deal gently and responsibly with their little partners.

PRACTICE IS ALWAYS BETTER than any theory. Are there already rats living in your house? Then the children are guaranteed to be enthusiastic when they are allowed to find out about the life and special traits of the little rodents—and at the same time get guidance in a nonthreatening manner on how to deal with them respectfully.

No Hubbub and No Noise

Sometimes children make noise and enjoy doing it. They can be frantic, and sometimes they can't sit still for ten seconds. Unfortunately rats don't like all this. Show your children how the animals react to different behaviors: Shouts, loud noises, and wild arm movements upset the cage dwellers; they remain on the other side of the cage or hide in the houses. Call gently to the rats, and crouch down in front of the cage to be at the same level as them. The children will see how one rat after another comes to the cage bars. Finally, find out together which call the little rodents come to more quickly: yours or the children's.

The Right Treatment

Explain to the children that rats are afraid of enemies from above, so they should never grab them from overhead. Also, they must not surprise the rats from behind, for they may bite from fear. Younger children under the age of six should not pick up rats; to the older ones you can demonstrate the proper carrying technique (see page 58). Resting times are taboo, and rats must never be disturbed when they are eating. Children certainly will understand that they have to take particular care with older animals.

Care

From the age of ten, children can take over feeding and cleaning the cage. The responsibility makes them proud, and the rats' trust is solidified. But keep an eye on the care so your animals get what they need.

Saying Good-bye

When a rat dies, the children should say good-bye. Also tell them why the rat died, and explain to them that their dear friend will always remain with them if they keep it in their memory and their heart.

Rats and the Law

The right to own a pet is restricted when a third party is unreasonably bothered or harmed and when the number of pets is limited by local ordinance.

Home Life

- Rental properties: If pet ownership is not generally prohibited in the rental contract, you need no permission from the landlord. Precedents confirm that the rats must cause no annoyance to other renters.
- Condominiums: The owner's association defines pet ownership and terms.

Consumer Law

Laws regulating pet purchase and health warranty vary by state. While no pet provider can guarantee absolute health, an obligation to sell a healthy pet remains. Any known infectious exposures or heritable or other disease must be exposed to a buyer. Breeders will often replace an unhealthy pet with another from their stock; they generally have no obligation to refund a purchase price in lieu of replacement, but some will. Purchase contracts define whether a breeder or store is responsibile for medical care for a preexisting problem.

Liability

Pet owners are liable for damages to people and property caused by their animals. Check your personal liability insurance contract to see if rats are covered.

1 **The way to a loving relationship is through the stomach.** The new rat dares to go through the open cage door for the first time and carefully sniffs the tantalizing treat offered by hand.

2 **A Sign of Trust.** As soon as the rat willingly climbs onto your open hand, you can slowly pick it up. Put it down immediately if it becomes restless and tries to climb out of your hand.

Six Steps Toward Trust

At first everything is strange. Give the animals time and put the open transport box into the cage. Soon your rats will inspect the new home and look for the food dish or water bottle. Building trust takes time and patience. You will reach the goal with these steps:

3. Friendship Treats. The prospect of tasty food hastens acquaintanceship. Keep offering treats by holding them in your open hand through the open cage door. Hand feeding, with certain exceptions, should be limited to such things as acclimating new animals and nursing sick animals back to health (see page 71). Otherwise the rat will quickly regard the person with the food as subordinate, since a dominant rat never offers food to its colleagues.

DID YOU KNOW THAT . . .

. . . male rats engage in boxing matches?

Even though an established pecking order is not immediately ascertainable in the pack, the males fight to see which one is the stronger. The combatants stand erect facing one another and strike the opponent with the front paws—just as boxers do. As a signal of surrender the loser assumes the posture of humility and lies on its back. Serious injuries are rare.

1. Awakening Curiosity. Get the rats used to your presence by staying near the cage and produce repeated, similar sounds or gentle calls. During this time it's best to wear the same clothing (and no head covering).

2. Sniff Test. It usually doesn't take long for curiosity to win out and for the animals to cease hiding. Hold your hand in the open cage door and wait until the residents get used to it and sniff it.

4. Stroke Test. As soon as the rat allows itself to be picked up, you can carefully and gently chuck it under the chin or stroke its back.

5. Elevation. Make a bowl with one hand and let the rat climb in. Use the other hand to support it on the side and lift up slowly. Put the rat down as soon as it becomes restless.

6. Sign of Trust. The ice is finally broken when the rat voluntarily comes to you, climbs onto your arm or shoulder, and gently nibbles your ear.

For Rats there is nothing greater than
free exercise in the house. You are responsible
for their safety, fun, and adventure.

Ten Rules for Exercise Outside the Cage

Rats are very active animals. Because the cage by itself can never satisfy their urge to move, the daily time outside the cage is a must. It also keeps the rats mentally fit, because there is something new to discover everywhere.

▸ Let the rats out of the cage for two hours a day, for example one hour in the morning and one in the evening.
▸ Permission to leave the cage is granted only to hand-tame animals.
▸ Never let the rats run free without supervision.
▸ During the time the rats are free the rat room is off-limits to all other animals in the house.
▸ Particularly early on, the terrain available to the travelers should be limited and easy to oversee.
▸ Make cracks, holes, and hiding places inaccessible, and close doors, windows, and drawers (see page 60).
▸ Keep to a set schedule for exercise outside the cage, preferably during the active phases in the morning and evening. Generally the rats will be waiting at the cage bars.
▸ Don't feed the rats until the excursion is over. Then the parolees will often return to the cage on their own. A door near the floor makes it easier to get back in.
▸ Never grab from above the rats that don't voluntarily return to the cage; rather, let them climb onto your hand or into a short tube (see page 60).

▸ If you set up a climbing tree or a playground in the room, you will have everything under the best possible control. A flowerpot weighted with stones provides a secure stand for the climbing tree, and small treats or pieces of fruit hanging in the tree (such as a whole apple) will provide fun for an extended time.

Drop by Drop

Rats use droplets of urine to mark territory, passageways, and everything they regard as possessions (and this includes trusted people). Restrict their exercise outside the cage to one room and cover sensitive surfaces and valuable furniture and textiles.

The rat holds its nose high in the air to sniff its surroundings.

Bookworms in the shelves: The parolees romp enthusiastically and with great endurance on the bookshelves during the daily exercise outside the cage. And in the process they thoroughly inspect every angle and corner.

A Rat-Proof House

Before your rats are let out of the cage, all the danger areas in the house must be "defused."

- The rats are allowed out only when the doors and windows are closed.
- Close all drawers and cabinets to keep an animal from being accidentally shut in. The same applies to the dryer, washing machine, and dishwasher.
- Wall sockets and electrical cords must be moved so they cannot be gnawed.
- Many plants are poisonous to rats (see page 71). If in doubt, remove them from the rat room.
- When the rats are free, tie up drapes and curtains. The animals' claws could get stuck in the fabric.
- Cracks (e.g., under cabinets and shelves) must be made inaccessible.
- Household cleansers, solvents, varnishes, and medications must be put away.
- Unplug hot plates and toasters. Keep the rats in their cage if you have burning candles or a fire in the fireplace.
- Foodstuffs and leftovers must be inaccessible to the rats.
- Close up trash and composting containers and remove plastic trash.
- Keep the rats out of the toilet and bathtub.
- Do not allow any other animals in the room while the rats are free.
- Move about carefully to avoid accidentally stepping on a rat.

One Still Got Away . . .

A rat has disappeared and won't come out of its hiding place:

- Hold treats in front of the hiding place; call to it in a gentle voice.
- Don't know where the animal is hiding? Set out dishes with food that can't be dragged away (such as mashed potatoes or yogurt). Sprinkle flour around the dishes so you can follow the tracks to the hiding place.

Help Wanted: Caretaker

You want to go away for a vacation, are traveling on business, or get sick. Of course your rats still need care during this time, preferably from a caregiver who has lots of experience dealing with the small mammals. So don't start your search a week before the vacation starts, but make contacts early and notify your chosen pet sitter early. You can get addresses of appropriate people from breeders, rat clubs, and your veterinarian. Sometimes you can also locate a neighbor or a friend who can become familiar with the cage dwellers before your absence.

Travel Only in an Emergency

Travel involves stress for the rats; they feel secure only in a familiar cage. If a trip can't be avoided (for example, to the veterinarian), the rat must always be inside a transport box (see Tip, page 50). If your animals have to stay in a different place for a fairly long time, they need a completely set-up cage. If a rat disappears in strange surroundings, it usually doesn't come back, so temporarily do away with the exercise outside the cage. Also: Negative reactions are not so rare nowadays when you show up in public with a rat. This does nothing to help the image of the little animals.

MY PET

How Important Am I to My Rats?

For rats the familiar person is far more than a food dispenser. The person is a part of the pack and will be treated with the same attention and love as their own colleagues. Some simple tests will show you how great this love is.

The Test Begins:
○ Do all the cage residents run expectantly to the bars as soon as I come into the room?
○ Do they react to my call—even when they are outside the cage?
○ Do they seek out physical contact with me and climb up on me?
○ Do they like to sit on my shoulder, and do they allow themselves to be carried around the house?
○ Do they nibble my ears and slip into jacket sleeves or breast pockets?

My Test Results:

A New Rat Moves In

Harmony and helpfulness characterize the cooperation in the rat pack. The animals recognize one another by their group-specific scent. Strange rats and ones that smell different are attacked and driven away. So in order to avoid fights, you must introduce a new rat to the old, established cage group very carefully and in several steps.

Not until the rat pack can **smell the new rat** can it move into their cage.

The Halfway House

Upon arrival the new rat should be kept in a separate cage, away from the other rats. Because it will be housed there for only a short time, the setup can be quite simple, but it must offer opportunities to climb and keep busy. Place the cage in view of the group cage (approximately 3 to 6 feet/2–3 m away) so that the animals can smell each other.

Hand Taming

Win the trust of the newcomer (see page 58). This provides the animal with security and facilitates further action.

Equipment Swap

A few items or toys from the setup are exchanged between the two cages. This is the easiest way to get all the animals used to the different smells.

Sniff Encounter

Outside both cages and ideally out of sight of the other animals, the first meeting takes place between the new rat and one member of the group on neutral ground. For the first sniff contact, select the most peaceful pack animal. Small fights are totally normal. The rats need to be separated only if the meeting triggers a serious fight and bite wounds become a danger. Be prepared for this emergency with some thick gloves. If everything comes off peacefully, gradually introduce the newcomer to all the group members.

A Change of Residence

After exchanging furniture both sides have become somewhat familiar with the scents and no longer find them entirely strange and threatening. So that the newcomer is eventually accepted without trouble by the group, lodge it for one day inside the pack's cage while the regular inhabitants temporarily make do with the second cage. After that everybody goes back to the regular homes.

Moving In

You have now done everything to avoid conflicts. Now comes the jump into the cold water: The new rat is placed into the large cage with the others. Stay close by so you can intervene if the integration goes awry. Naturally the excitement is high, and many hackles are raised. But oftentimes new and old rats cuddle after a short time, as if things had never been any other way.

1 **New and solo.** A new rat comes into the house and initially has its own cage.

The first sniff contact. The new rat and the most peaceable **2** ▶ one of the group meet on neutral ground outside the cage. Usually the ice is quickly broken after some intensive sniffing.

◀ **3** **A change of residence.** To get both sides used to the strange smells, the new rat moves into the main cage for a day, and the group lodges in the second cage for a short time.

Welcome! The big day has arrived: The new rat can finally **4** ▶ move in with the group in the large cage. This rarely comes off without some excitement, but after a short while they are bosom buddies.

Questions About
Purchase, Acclimation, and Living Conditions

? Rats don't see very well. So I was surprised when a friend recommended that I not change clothes too often during the acclimation period. Can the animals even tell the difference?
When you are so close to the rats that they can pick up your scent, your appearance is of no importance. But at a distance the rats react especially to the silhouette: If you suddenly appear before the cage in a coat instead of a T-shirt, it's no wonder that the animals feel insecure. It's even clearer if you "disguise" yourself with a cap or a hat. On the other hand, a shirt that smells of rat fosters trust among the new animals. And you should not be wearing your Sunday suit when the troupe climbs up on you. Rats mark everything they consider their property with droplets of urine (see page 59). And this includes you.

? Evidently there are some rat owners who simply let "excess" rats go because they are convinced that they will make out all right on their own. Is this justified?
This is not justified. Pets rarely survive in the wild and may introduce disease to the native population. Breeders and pet stores will often accept return of rats purchased from them. Alternatively, locate a humane shelter or other rat owner to care for rats in need of a home.

? I don't know much about rats. Is it worthwhile to visit a small-mammal show, or should I get my information from someplace else?
A visit of this type is a good idea in any case. At markets and shows you can take a look at more animals than anywhere else and make comparisons. The exhibitors are primarily breeders, from whom you can get valuable practical tips and contact information. When and where small-mammal shows take place is usually advertised in the local pages of daily newspapers and on the Internet. But you can also find out the dates from the sponsoring clubs.

? My rats are very friendly. But sometimes I get nipped sharply on a finger, especially on first contact. How come?
I am quite sure that this is merely a bite test after you have been handling rat food. Rats are primarily nose creatures. And since your hand smells so deceptively like delicious food, it may sometimes happen that a rat will bite it. Avoid such misunderstandings by washing your hands after preparing the food (but don't use scented soap or perfumed lotion). With new and shy animals, rub your hands with bedding before making contact so that you have the trusted hutch smell.

Will it be easier for the rats to get to know each other if I place the cage with a new rat right beside the group cage?

Under no circumstances should you do this. The closeness causes both sides to act aggressively and continually threaten one another. Place the two cages 6 to 10 feet (2–3 m) apart. The animals can see each other and slowly get used to the smells. Even then it will take some time for the excitement to die down.

I would like to have a group of three females. How can I be sure that I'm not buying a pregnant female at the pet shop?

Buying an animal in a pet shop is a question of trust, as it is with a breeder. Before purchasing, make contact with other rat owners or respondents at a rat club. People will almost always give you addresses of reliable pet shops.

Female rats give birth to their offspring after twenty to twenty-four days. Unfortunately, the symptoms of pregnancy (swollen teats, thick stomach, nesting activity) first become evident only a few days before birth. A rat breeder intentionally mates females and males. Here there is no risk of undesired pregnancy.

Our rat cage is in the living room. I am a smoker and spend several hours a day in this room. Is this harmful to the rats?

Cigarette smoke is equally harmful to animals and humans and places a strain on the lungs. In addition, rats are particularly susceptible to respiratory diseases. Draft and very dry or polluted air are the most common causes of disease.

When the rats are outside their cage, I set up a small climbing tree for them. But my four rats prefer to climb on the bookshelf. Should I allow this?

The main thing is that you always keep an eye on your little rascals, and that none of them disappear under the bookshelf. Also make sure that no exposed electrical cords pass through the bookshelf, and that the "mountain climbers" don't latch on to unstable items like vases and figurines and go crashing to the floor with them.

How long does it take rats to get used to a new home and owners?

Rats are individualists. Self-assured characters may let themselves be petted after three or four days, but shy animals sometimes will still vanish into their hiding place after two weeks when the owner approaches the cage.

The Best Food
for Your Rats

The "rat motor" always operates at high rpms and needs
high-quality fuel: a balanced commercial diet and fresh, vitamin-rich
fruits and vegetables every day.

A Varied and
Healthy Diet

Rats eat and digest everything: This is not true for wild rats, and certainly not true for domesticated rats. But not everything that is edible is good for the rodents. The owner's duty is to feed the rats a balanced and healthy diet.

IT'S IN THE MIX A quality commercial rat diet is an ideal base food. Just as we don't want to eat precisely the same soup day in and day out, our rodents also need a tasty and varied mix of foods, including everything that will keep them healthy and fit.

The Forgotten Heritage

For rats living in the wild, the search for food is a very toilsome and tricky business. If the pack finally discovers a new source of food, it must not simply fill its collective belly: The strange food could be inedible or even poisoned. Caution and suspicion are called for (see page 75). The sheltered associates inside the cage don't have to keep struggling with this. After many generations of communal life with humans, they have learned to trust their "food master" implicitly, and they accept even unfamiliar food without hesitation. The love that passes through the stomach on the way to the heart is a show of trust. But it also places the owner in a position of responsibility. For the owner is the only one who can assure the proper nutrition for the animals.

Quality Foods Build Strength

Just like high-performance athletes, the continually active rats need a basic diet that will provide strength and be easily digested. Start with a high-quality commercial rat diet. Rodent lab block can be too high in fat for a pet's diet. The advantage of prepared food is that it assembles a number of nutritional components that provide important nutrients, vitamins, and minerals, and it is pleasing to the button-eyed clientele. Among others, this includes rice, wheat, soybean, flax, corn, oats, and alfalfa. Because rats need a certain portion of

Grains are the main component of prepared mixes. ▶

2 **Food for Gnawing.** Rats love hard bread, crisp breads, and zwieback. Gnawing these foods also wears down the incisors, which grow continuously.

1 **Always Fresh.** Old, stale drinking water is replaced every day. Water bottles are a better choice for the cage than water bowls.

3 **A Cheese Treat.** Cheese and other animal foods should be provided only in small portions and on an irregular basis.

protein in their diet (see facing page), prepared mixtures usually also include fish or meat, perhaps in pellet form. But not every rat likes the pellets, so sometimes they get left in the dish.

You can give your rodents prepared food with meat as a sole food source. But prepared food mixes for hamsters and guinea pigs are not appropriate for rats.

Fruits and Vegetables

Apples, bananas, pears, peaches, and cherries (with pits removed), melons, figs, pineapple, grapes, and kiwis, plus red beets, carrots, peas, cucumbers, chicory, zucchini, asparagus, peppers, and many other types of fruits and vegetables are healthy foods for the little gourmands. In addition, rats like herbs such as chickweed, parsley, and freshly picked dandelion greens.

Important: Before serving fruits and vegetables, wash them in lukewarm water and dry them. Then cut them into small pieces. Feed only cooked potatoes. With seed foods, remove the shells and husks, which contain hydrocyanic acids. Raisins are fattening, but if fed must not be sulfurated.

Always Enough in the Dish

Rats use up lots of energy because they are always in motion, and they have a high metabolism. This means that the rodents need food regularly and at frequent intervals. A lack of food for even five to six hours can cause circulatory problems. A longer period of fasting inevitably leads to serious problems (perhaps even to collapse); for this reason you should never force a day of fasting even on overweight animals.

Fruits and a balanced commercial diet must always be available in the rat cage: A slightly heaping soupspoon of a balanced commercial diet covers the daily requirement of an adult animal of average size; very large or hyperactive rats will polish off twice as much, however. Cut back on the daily ration only if there is always leftover food in the dish and the animals stockpile a lot.

Small Portions of Animal-Based Food

Rats cannot get by without a supplement of animal-based food. But feed it only sparingly; an excess can lead to allergies and skin problems, and the animals probably will become more susceptible to cancers as well. This can be a hard-boiled egg, some favorite yogurt (with no fruit additives), a spoonful of cottage cheese, a little fish or meat (both cooked), or a small piece of mild, hard cheese. The cage bunch will be excited by the tasty special rations. But that should not tempt you to give your rodents a second helping.

Nice Things You Can Do for Your Pets

▸ Freshly sprouted seeds are tasty and rich in vitamins. Shops sell prepared sprout mixtures, but you can also grow sprouts from parakeet food. This is easiest to do in a sprouter (from a pet shop or a health food store). The first sprouts appear after no more than two days. Especially in the winter months, sprout food provides variety to the menu, but it doesn't replace other fresh foods. And sprouts cannot be stored long, for they mold quickly.

▸ A small treat from the hand and your rats will love you all the more. And just as hand feeding should not be the rule (see page 71), treats should be the exception, especially fattening foods such as nuts, yogurt and vitamin drops containing sugar, and sunflower seeds. Good choices include dried fruit (berries, and banana and apple chips), millet, coconut, pieces of dried carrots, and heads of grains. Particularly good choices are chew sticks and corncobs, which are fun to gnaw and give the rats something to do. All rats also lick their paws over vitamin paste and cheese from a tube. But just like baby food, these are primarily important energy sources for sick and weak animals.

TIP

Bite by Bite

Rats go to the food dish several times a day and always have only small meals. Their small stomachs can hold no more than ½ ounce (15 ml). So don't clean up presumed leftovers right away, but give the animals time to eat. Remove leftover food after a maximum of twenty-four hours.

Zwieback, Twigs, and Dog Biscuits

Hard food for hard teeth: There must always be something to gnaw in the rat cage to keep the continually growing rodent teeth worn down: crisp breads and whole-kernel bread, dog biscuits, old pieces of bread, and zwieback. The rats will spend lots of time gnawing

removed; corn food, for example, gets contaminated from droppings or wet from urine.

Fresh Water

Drinking water must always be available—preferably in two water bottles. Empty out the leftover water daily and fill the bottles with fresh water. Clean the sipper tubes once a week with hot water.

DID YOU KNOW THAT . . .

. . . cecal droppings are vitally important to rats?

When rats (like rabbits) eat their own droppings, it is a normal behavior. Rats form two different types of droppings: a softer one, and another that is nearly dry and hard. The soft droppings contain vitamins and bacteria, without which the rodents' nutritional requirements cannot be met. Thus, even rats that are fed a balanced, healthy diet ingest up to 65 percent of the cecal droppings. With dietary deficiencies, the percentage is even higher. If eating the droppings is stopped—for example, by keeping the rats on a wire floor—signs of malnutrition set in. Baby rats consume their mother's droppings from the fifteenth to the twenty-eighth day of life. In conjunction with the mother's milk, this creates an immunity against a dangerous infection of the digestive tract. Young animals need the cecal droppings to form the proper bacteria.

fresh twigs from unsprayed fruit trees, beech, birch, and other deciduous trees.

Cleaning Out the Stockpiles

Regularly inspect and empty the food stores inside the cage. Leftovers from succulent and green foods must also be

Even though rats accept many sources of food, they are **anything but garbage eaters;** they need a proper balanced diet.

Other Things You Should Know About Feeding

A few types of fruits and vegetables are less beneficial, and others are completely indigestible. You should know the most important ones, plus the houseplants that are poisonous to rodents.

Even Rats Cannot Digest Everything

▸ Provide only in small quantities: berries and citrus fruits (very acidic), all types of cabbage (produce gas), cheese and yogurt (lots of protein), sunflower seeds and nuts (fatty and fattening), lettuce (high nitrate content).
▸ Taboo for the food dish: raw potatoes and beans, raw eggs, onions, sulfured dried fruits, cow's milk (contains lactose), spicy foods, moldy cheese, leftover foods.

Poisonous Plants

Plants that are poisonous to rats include cyclamen, amaryllis, azalea, Christmas rose, chrysanthemum, dieffenbachia, ivy, geranium, hydrangea, hyacinth, crocus, lily of the valley, mistletoe, narcissus, primrose, oleander, and poinsettia. For safety, remove unknown plants from the rat room.

Good Table Manners

When rats eat, they usually sit in the characteristic posture on their haunches and with an arched back. That way their paws are free and they can very nimbly hold and twist and turn the pieces of food. After every meal the rodents clean themselves thoroughly: They don't like leftover food on their nose and the facial hairs. There are rarely conflicts over food, but the animals keep a minimum distance from their messmates. And with special treats they prefer to withdraw into a corner.

Hand Feeding

Hand-fed rats become tame more quickly, but otherwise only sick and old animals, which need to be persuaded to eat, should be fed by hand. Runaway animals can often be lured into coming back with a treat held in front of the hiding place.

Bad idea: Many plants are poisonous to rats and have no place in the rat room.
▾

Rules for Proper, Healthy Feeding

An overview of the most important points in feeding: What must you keep in mind while feeding? What do rats like? How do you avoid unbalanced feeding? And when should the rats be fed?

Providing a Daily Ration. Check to see if everything gets eaten. If there regularly are leftovers in the dish and lots of food gets hoarded, the daily ration should be reduced. The basic ration of a balanced commercial diet is one level tablespoon per day, but many animals need two.

Cleaning Up Food Stockpiles. Rats store up supplies in all possible and impossible places in the cage. Empty the depots daily to keep mold and disease organisms from getting in.

Away with the Leftovers. Remove left-over food from the cage after no more than twenty-four hours. This applies especially for all fruits and vegetables that spoil quickly, and to seed foods that are contaminated or soaked with urine.

Leave the Cecal Droppings. Rats usu-ally re-ingest the cecal droppings (see page 70). In their absence symptoms of malnutrition may appear.

Fresh Drinking Water. Fill the water bottles with fresh water every day. Water must always be available.

Clean Dishes. Before feeding, clean the dishes under hot water.

Food Games. Searching for hidden food keeps the rodents vitally interested and physically fit (see page 74). Noodles (cooked or raw) are perfect for a "tug-of-war," and the prospect of tasty morsels in the digging box often tempts several animals to dig all at once.

No Fasting. Never let your rats go hun-gry. They eat only small meals, but on the average they go to the food dish every two hours.

Everything Always Fresh. Fruit and dried vegetables that are going bad or molding are harmful and are a threat to the rats' health.

Healthy Treats. Spoil the rats with ears of corn, carrot chips, or dried apples instead of high-calorie, sugary snacks that will make them fat.

Nursing Sick Animals. Power bars and similar calorie bombs are only for sick and weak rats.

Safe at Home. Always feed right after the rats have been outside the cage. Then the rodents will generally come back to the cage voluntarily.

Under Control. Regularly observe your rat society when they eat. That is the only way to see if one animal is getting shortchanged, or if anyone is greedy, or even refusing to eat.

Sweet Tooth. Many rats eat only their favorite tidbits and leave everything else untouched. To prevent imbalanced nutrition, refill the dish only when the other food gets eaten.

Mealtimes. It's best to feed your rats in the morning and the evening.

Hard Food. Materials for gnawing must always be available, such as crisp bread, crackers, chew sticks, and twigs.

In the Middle. Don't place the food dishes right up against the cage bars, because this is where the residents like to run.

Hand Feeding. You should hand feed only animals that need help with accli-mation, and old or sick rats.

Proper Feeding
at a Glance

Working for Food

Hide treats and pieces of bread under roots, inside tubes, under straw, and in the digging box, or hang a whole apple on the climbing tree. Searching for the food is fun for the rodents and keeps them physically fit.

◀ Healthy and Delicious

Fruits, vegetables, and herbs are on the daily menu. A small piece of melon tastes good and provides important vitamins. Carrots and slices of cucumber are the right choice for fitness and a good figure.

◀ Daily Ration

One level tablespoon of a balanced commercial diet per animal per day is the rule of thumb. But many rats will need significantly more. The rations should be cut back if leftovers regularly appear in the food dish.

Hearty Nibbling ▶

There is always room in the tummy for a crunchy crisp bread. Although fruit and other succulent leftover food should be removed promptly, dry food can stay in the cage a little longer.

▲ Clean Drinking Containers

The drinking water in the bottles must be replaced every day. At least once a week the sipper tubes must be cleaned thoroughly with a brush, and the functioning of the dispensers must be checked.

Fitness for Rats with a Sweet Tooth

Rats like to play, climb, and dig to earn their living. And they are constantly searching for anything edible. What could be more logical than encouraging their mind and body on a search for tasty munchies? The reward comes free.

SIMPLE IS BORING Rats are clever; they have an infallible sense of direction and know every corner of their cage. To really get them going, you have to dish up some tough nuts to crack in the games of search.

The Food Course

A treat placed under the swing, in a cage corner, or on the roof of a house is no challenge for a rat. For a course with some exceptional hiding places for food,

What's that neat smell? Every rat stands tall for a treat.

the motto is "the more complicated the better." Give your imagination free rein.

▶ For digging: Place banana chips among the scraps of newspaper in the digging box, or hide walnuts (with shells) in the straw.

▶ For gathering: make trails of pumpkin seeds or beans on steps and ramps, and fruit drops inside the running tubes.

▶ For climbing: Hang dried apple rings on the knots of the climbing rope; hang a dried corncob or a whole apple on the climbing tree; attach spaghetti to the cross ropes.

▶ For unwrapping: Provide nuts or dried berries wrapped in paper.
  Combine search tasks that require the animals to use a variety of skills. Help from you generally is needed only in the beginning.

▶ Build in fixed "training times" for the food games, preferably during the morning or evening activity phases. Your rats will immediately figure out what's on the schedule.

▶ You can get the rats excited about a search even when they are outside the cage. The new hiding places are a special challenge. But put out only very small food rewards so the rats are hungry enough to return to the cage for the main meal.

MY PET

Who Has the Sharpest Nose?

Searching for food is in the blood of even tame rats. By always providing new hiding places for food, you keep your rats on their toes, encourage lots of exercise and physical fitness, and turn them into enthusiastic playmates. Who is the champion?

The Test Begins:

○ For beginners: Place the treats in the open next to a root, under the stairs, or in a tube. The rat that's one step ahead gets the treat.
○ For advanced rats: Hide the morsels of food or pieces of fruit in the digging box.
○ For experts: The treats hang from a rope like bird food or from the cover of the cage.
  For pros: The treat is hidden inside one of three boxes with (sliding) covers.

My Test Results:

How Rats Test Food

Rats living in the wild are always on the search for food. If they are very hungry, they often have no choice but to try unknown food sources. Then one member of the pack usually samples a couple of bites of the unknown food. When the test eater returns to the group, the others sniff its muzzle and test its breath and perhaps even its saliva. Both evidently supply important information about the ingredients and the taste of the food. Only then is it decided if all the rats can eat the food. This special form of communication also forms food preferences that are spread within the pack and to offspring. There are no special tasters that are chosen by their colleagues and sent out to test foods—even though there are stubborn reports of such sacrificial behaviors. If the rats cannot tolerate a certain food, they avoid it for a long time, even forever. Even in the case of poisoned bait the animals are quick to associate cause and effect.

As trust of humans among pet rats has increased, mistrust and caution have continually decreased. Even with unknown food in the dish, they usually don't need a second invitation—provided the offering meets their taste requirements.

Questions About
Food and Feeding

? Can I strengthen my rats' fitness and immune defenses if I occasionally give them a vitamin and mineral preparation?

A balanced food mixture contains everything that the rodents need, including vitamins and minerals. But nutritional supplements can be important in the case of sick animals, expectant or nursing mothers, and young animals: In these exceptional cases you need to discuss the type and amount of the food supplement with a veterinarian. Foods containing vitamin C are not necessary as a supplement, for the rats' body produces this vitamin by itself.

? There is less fresh fruit in the winter. Is canned fruit an appropriate substitute?

Most groceries provide enough fruit variety, even in winter, to continue offering your rats fresh fruit. If you need alternatives, rats will like canned pineapple and peaches just as much as fresh fruit. But you should provide the canned food less frequently and in smaller portions, since it almost always contains lots of sugar. A good alternative is frozen fruits and vegetables. They are a year-round source of everything that the rats' heart and stomach crave. If you want to provide more variety in the food dish, offer your rodents fresh sprouted food (see page 69) or grow a few herbs in a pot.

? The ball valve in the water bottle was stuck and the rats couldn't get any water. Fortunately I noticed it in time. How can this be prevented?

Use safety in numbers by providing a second water bottle. Water bottles should be standard equipment in every rat cage so that there is always enough drinking water available. Also test the functioning of the water dispensers regularly; this is easy to do during the weekly cleaning of the sipping tubes.

? Several of my rowdies often pull and tug on a favorite treat and claim it for themselves. Can this lead to real trouble?

Of course every rat wants to have a treat for itself, especially when treats are not always available. But real food envy rarely occurs in the pack. If one rat eventually gets the upper hand, it brings its prize to a safe place and savors a couple of bites. Then the treat is again made available to the others. Often two or three animals will gnaw on a large bit of food (such as a cone) at the same time without any stress. They merely keep a minimal distance from one another. Even a tug-of-war with a noodle comes off peacefully. Best yet: The two opponents get to work on their physical fitness.

Why do the rodent teeth keep growing? Isn't this a mistake in the blueprint?

Quite the contrary. With their powerful bite and durable, sharp incisors, rodents can use food sources that are unavailable to other animals. The rodent teeth, which have no roots and grow continually, are automatically kept short, and they sharpen themselves, for only the front surface is covered with very hard enamel. A rat's rodent teeth grow more than ½ inch (1 cm) in a month. Within a short time the hard food would quickly render unusable teeth that didn't grow continually. The success of this situation is proven by the fact that rodents (*Rodentia*) make up the largest order of mammals, and today more than half of all mammals are rodents.

Must rat food contain animal protein? Other small mammals such as guinea pigs get along fine without it.

Animal protein is essential for the rats' health. This is particularly true of the offspring. If this protein is not present in the food for the young, they grow noticeably more slowly. However, providing too much protein in the food increases the susceptibility to skin diseases, and perhaps even to cancers.

One of my rats has a decidedly favorite sport: sleeping and eating. Is it harmful for it to have a little too much meat on its ribs?

Rats are strong animals, but they should be slender. Otherwise there may be a vicious circle: A rat that's fat becomes sedentary, and if it doesn't get enough exercise, it puts on more weight. It has been shown that over-weight rats have a shorter life expectancy. You have to be particularly careful with older animals, whose taste for exercise usually declines. A rule of thumb is that one slightly rounded tablespoon of a balanced commercial diet per day is adequate for a healthy grown and normally active rat, plus sufficient fruits and vegetables. You should get your lazybones moving with some games and sports. It would also make sense to reduce its daily ration slightly, but this is difficult to do when rats are kept in a group.

Can I provide commercially available cat grass for my rats?

Many rats really like freshly sprouted cat grass, but you should not make it available all the time. Rodent grass, which you can likewise grow, consists of different types of grass, and it appeals to many rats.

Proper Care and
Good Health

Rats are exceptionally clean animals and rarely get sick.
The owner is responsible for keeping their home clean—and
simultaneously practicing important health precautions.

Introduction to Care and Cage Cleaning

Caring for rats is a package deal that includes not only protecting against diseases and cleaning the cage, but also providing the right living conditions—from nutrition and ways to keep active to daily attention from the owner.

TWENTY MINUTES A DAY Feeding, cleaning up leftovers, changing the drinking water, and cleaning the toilet are part of the daily care routine. For an easily accessible and practical rat cage you barely need to spend twenty minutes a day. In the process you can take care of the morning visit, and take a look at the rats' state of health and the behavior of the entire troupe (see pages 80–81) without much effort.

Proper Care and Living Conditions

All caregiving measures are effective only if the living conditions are also correct. These include the following:

▶ Cage size: The construction and dimensions of the cage are keyed to the number of inhabitants. If it is too small or too low, social conflicts are inevitable, and the animals become stressed out. In addition, a cage that is too small quickly becomes dirty.

▶ Location: A noisy, hectic environment makes rats nervous and sick in the long run. Draft and frequent temperature fluctuations weaken their defenses. Mental fitness suffers when the cage is relegated to a dark,

isolated corner, where the animals can't take part in the life going on around them.

▶ Nutrition: A balanced, appropriate food is a guarantee for stable health. Only healthy rats groom themselves regularly and thus practice preventive health care. Overweight animals that are fed an excessively rich diet neglect this care.

▶ Things to do: Boredom makes rats sick. Rats are intelligent, active animals. They languish when there is nothing to do or there are no games to play. In addition, daily exercise outside the cage is essential.

Lots of Wash: ▶
The routine for rats includes grooming several times a day. They not only wash behind their ears, but also meticulously wash every part of their body.

▶ Affection: The trusted owner is considered a member of the pack. Closeness and physical contact with the owner increase the rodents' sense of well-being and gives them a feeling of security and safety.

Marking Is Part of It

The cage dwellers get used to a toilet dish rather easily. But housebreaking attempts have no effect on the droplets of urine with which the rats mark out their own territory. Marking the territory and all the items that are considered to be the property of the pack (including even the owner) is part of the rodents' hereditary behavior and cannot be changed by any training measures. Because the rats also use urine marking for orientation, their time outside the cage should be restricted to one room in which there are no furnishings with valuable, sensitive surfaces.

Looking Spiffy

Rats generally don't need any help with grooming. They groom and wash themselves thoroughly and persistently, especially after meals, principally on their face and behind their ears. The toes and claws are also gnawed regularly and made free of particles of dirt. If care is neglected, it is often an early symptom of illness.

The Morning Visit

The rat owner's daily health inspection of the charges is a given. Usually the appearance is a sufficient indicator. Take every change in physical appearance and behavior seriously and investigate or observe it. The motto "Wait and see if things get better" doesn't work with rats. Illnesses often come on very quickly with them. So in case of any doubt, visit the veterinarian. Here's what to look for in the morning visit:
▶ Body: sides not sunken in
▶ Posture: no cowering or sharply arched back
▶ Head position: normal and level
▶ Movement: without restriction
▶ Fur: free of scabs and bald spots, no continual licking and scratching
▶ Eyes: clear and with no discharge
▶ Nose: clean, no secretions
▶ Anus: not soiled

◀ *A little wellness for rodent fur: A sand bath is beneficial. The fine sand not only removes annoying particles of dirt, but also gives the coat a new sheen.*

▸ Claws: not split or torn
▸ Droppings check: normal shape, no diarrhea, anus not matted
▸ Appetite: normal; the accustomed food is eaten without hesitation
▸ Breathing: noiseless
▸ Behavior: alert and not shy, lethargic, or withdrawn
▸ Behavior: lively and active, but not noticeably restless
▸ Affection: trusting of the owner, not withdrawn
▸ Physical contact: no signs of discomfort or defensive biting when touched

Trimming the Claws

With old and sick animals it sometimes happens that the claws don't wear down sufficiently. When they become too long, they must be trimmed carefully. Because there are blood vessels in the base of the claws, only the tip must be trimmed; otherwise the claw may bleed. Claw care is best done with two people: One holds the rat's body with one hand and the foot in the other; the second person trims. Fingernail clippers work well. And if a nail bleeds, rub it against a bar of soap, apply styptic powder, or apply continuous pressure with a cloth.

Sand Beautifies

A bowl with bird or chinchilla sand is a temptation to take a bath. A sand bath is part of comfort behavior. It not only provides clean fur, but also increases the sense of well-being. Because the sand gets dirty quickly, the bowl should not be left in the cage.

CHECKLIST

Daily Housecleaning

The rats quickly get used to the cleaning of the cage as long as it is always done at the same time and in the same order.

○ Remove leftovers: Before feeding, remove leftover fruits and vegetables, plus seeds that have become moist with urine or smeared with droppings.

○ Check the daily ration: Reduce the amount of food if there is regularly too much left in the food dishes.

○ Clean the food dishes: Rinse under hot water, using no soap or detergent.

○ Change the water: Empty out old drinking water and fill the water dispensers with fresh water.

○ Clean the toilet dish or corner: Replace soiled, damp bedding; replace the entire bedding if it is extremely dirty.

○ Put in new litter: Replace the bedding in heavily soiled areas.

○ Empty the storage areas: Remove hoarded food, e.g., from the houses and deposits buried in the bedding.

○ Check the latch on the cage: It is no trouble to check the stability of the setup while doing the cleaning.

Regularly cleaning the cage and accessories is the
best preventive health measure you can use
to protect your charges.

Essential: Hand Taming

The most important requirement for care and prevention is the trust that the cage dweller has for its owner (see page 58): All creatures should be hand tame and should let themselves be picked up and held without going on the defensive.

Water Games

Even though nearly all rats like water, there are individual differences, and in addition to real water rats there are also some stubborn nonswimmers. So always put in only enough water in the

Once a month should be a major cage cleaning, during which time the pets are let out.
▼

bathing basin so that the animals can still stand securely. Of course the water games go on only under your supervision. Also, the splashing pool is not part of the basic equipment, and it should not even be inside the cage; otherwise the entire bedding will get soaked.

Cleaning the Cage

▶ Make the cleaning easy by buying a cage and accessories made from materials that are easy to clean and can be wiped off easily. Large front doors and additional hatches provide good accessibility. For thorough cleaning the furnishings should come out without much hassle.

▶ Rats have an infallible sense of time. It generally takes just a couple of days for them to learn the feeding and cleaning times, and often they will be waiting for you at the cage bars. A stable daily routine also helps in acclimating new and shy animals. So tinker around with the cage only when the rats are awake and active, and never during their sleep phases.

▶ For cleaning, use hot water or a weak solution of vinegar and water, but no chemical cleaning agents. They get into the creatures' sensitive respiratory passages and harm their health.

▶ Every day remove leftover food, clean the toilet, and replace damp bedding in the toilet corner. Clean the food dishes with hot water.

▸ Every week replace the soiled straw, rinse out the water dispensers with hot water, change all the toilet straw, empty the food stockpiles, and replace the expendable materials (such as hay and newspaper).

▸ Every month (depending on degree of cleanliness, and even sooner with large groups), change all the bedding and clean the bottom pan with hot water or vinegar and water. Also wash off the floorboards, wipe down the bars of the cage, and wash or replace

Everybody Out on Cleaning Day

In order to have free access to everything during the monthly major cleaning, you should let your rats out of the cage during this time. To keep from losing track of large groups and having to look for strays later on, let them out in shifts of two or three at a time. Move the others into a second cage.

DID YOU KNOW THAT . . .

. . . rats cannot vomit?

A rat's stomach is divided by a fold. This anatomical feature means that the rodents cannot vomit. Rats sometimes can even deal with spoiled food that would be absolutely indigestible or harmful to humans. But they do not have the ability to expel toxic substances or foreign bodies, as we humans do in many instances. A rat can suffocate on a swallowed object. If you find yourself having to deal with this emergency, you must act immediately and boldly: Lift the animal by its hind legs and pat it not too timidly on the back until the foreign body comes loose and the rat can breathe freely again. A veterinarian has to consider the lack of a vomit reflex before performing an operation: People have to fast before an operation, but this would be unnecessary, and potentially harmful, to a rat.

all fabric covers on hammocks and swings. Items made of untreated wood in particular quickly soak up urine. They must be scrubbed energetically with a brush under hot water.

A Little Barn Smell

When you clean the cage, leave a couple of places untreated. The trusted barn smell means home to the inhabitants. It also keeps the animals from scent marking everywhere to identify their territory after the cleaning.

Keeping Rats Healthy

An intact pack society, appropriate accommodations, good nutrition, regular activity, and affection from the human: Do your rats have all of this? Then you have created the best basis for keeping your animals healthy.

TOUGHER THAN THEY'RE CRACKED UP TO BE: Rats are tough. But usually this is evident only with the wild brown rats, and not their domesticated relatives. On the contrary: As descendants from laboratory rats, pet rats are often considered sensitive and susceptible to diseases. But that is not true: Rats in a house do not fall sick more frequently than animals living in the wild. The fact that older rats become sick more frequently than their younger counterparts and suffer from specific age-related symptoms applies equally to both groups. At two to three years, their life expectancy is also essentially the same. Senior citizens aged five or six are found only among pet rats.

TIP

Never by the Tail or the Neck

Even though it is continually recommended, unfortunately, you should never pick up a rat by its tail. Grasping this sensitive body part is very painful for many animals, and the risk of injury is high; in the worst case the tail can even break off. Grasping by the neck is also inappropriate.

Early Detection Is the Best Life Insurance

As with many other small mammals, rats are characterized as having a high metabolism. The result is that illnesses can progress quickly. So as a rat owner, take every suspected illness seriously. Don't wait for physical alterations and noticeable changes in behavior; rather, when in doubt immediately consult a veterinarian. To be ready for this from the first day as a new rat owner, you should make contact with a veterinarian who has experience in dealing with small mammals even before your charges move in.

How to Protect Your Rats from Illness

What applies to humans also applies to rats: Prevention is the best remedy. If the living conditions satisfy the following eleven points, the animals are protected as effectively as possible against diseases.

1. A Strong Community. Rats are highly social creatures, and they quickly languish without constant contact with other rats. Young rats that are kept alone experience isolation stress, and their development is delayed. As adult animals, they exhibit abnormal behaviors that cannot be remedied.

▲

Never alone is the main thing: The proximity of colleagues gives rats a sense of security, reduces stress, and keeps them healthy.

2. Clean Living Quarters. Regular cage cleaning protects the inhabitants from disease pathogens and parasites. The frequency depends on how dirty it gets and the size of the group. In the presence of excess droppings and urine-soaked accessories, inadequate cleaning can produce vapors that harm the bronchi of the rats. The contamination of the air in the cage with ammonia is particularly critical.

3. Rest Area. Even in the most peaceful group there can be some stress. Then a rat must be able to pull back from communal living for a while. Houses and hiding places are the proper retreats.

4. The Right Climate. Rats are most comfortable at temperatures of 68–75°F (20–25°C) and humidity of 50 to 60 percent. Effective ventilation keeps odors from building up. Important: Draft is poison to rats and the most common cause of respiratory problems (see page 88).

5. Fresh Water. Water is the elixir of life for rats, too. Even when they get plenty of succulent foods, drinking water must always be present. Fill the water dispensers with fresh water every day. If the tap water is highly chlorinated, use bottled water.

6. Dental Care. Fruit tree twigs, old, hard bread, and untreated wood keep the rodent teeth short.

7. Good Nutrition. Balanced nutrition with a grain-based balanced commercial diet, succulent foods, and a small portion of animal-based food provides the basis for fitness and stable health.

8. Appropriate Portion Sizes. Fat rats are sluggish. A lack of exercise and being overweight contribute to circulatory problems and skin diseases. Cut back on the daily ration if there commonly are leftovers in the food dish and the rodents are piling up large stockpiles.

9. Games and Sports. Rats have to keep busy. With a little imagination you can turn the cage into an adventure land with stimulating games and gymnastic apparatuses.

10. Daily Exercise. Even a large cage is no substitute for a run outside the cage every day. The rats need to go on journeys of discovery for the benefit of their body and mind.

11. Cuddling. Trust and physical contact with people provide security and strengthen the immune defenses.

Security and warmth: Physical contact is very important for rats.

▼

Weight Loss Alarm

Weight loss is an alarm signal and often the initial symptom of an illness. Check a rat's weight if you suspect that it has grown thinner. You should also weigh all animals that show symptoms that cannot immediately be ascribed, such as apathetic behavior, unkempt fur, hair loss, or refusal to eat. Remember that the body weight is not significant unto itself—there can be major differences among rats. It's much more important to note if and how the weight changes.

Things That Make Rats Sick

Here are the most common mistakes in keeping and feeding rats:

▸ Cage: wrong location, too small, too low, or too little surface area, improper setup, no intermediate floors, lack of houses and hiding places, inadequate cleanliness, faulty ventilation

▸ Living conditions: living alone, stress in the group (domination by other rats), isolation stress in young animals, continuous disturbances during rest periods, no opportunities to play and keep busy

▸ Nutrition: overfeeding, too much animal protein, too many treats, spoiled or moldy succulent food, stale drinking water, dirty food dishes and bottle nipples, lack of materials to gnaw, leftovers from human food

▸ Exercise: infrequent or totally nonexistent

TYPICAL SYMPTOMS OF ILLNESS IN RATS

SYMPTOM	DESCRIPTION	CAUSES
Weight Loss	The rat loses around an ounce (20 g) of weight per week.	General disease symptom; malnutrition, parasites
Defensive Biting	A previously trusting animal refuses to be picked up and is nippy.	The rat is in pain, and every touch hurts it.
Apathy	The rat is totally inactive and sits apathetically in the corner.	Symptom of serious illness; get to the veterinarian right away.
Breathing Problems	Sneezing, shallow breathing, rattling noise while breathing	Respiratory illness
Discharge from Eye or Nose	Reddish secretion from corner of eye and nose, inflamed eyes	General symptom of illness; stress, parasites, improper living conditions
Hard Abdomen	Distended, tense abdomen, reduced food intake	Damp, improper, or too much food
Diarrhea	Matted, soiled anal area; weak and inactive	Stomach-intestinal illness; faulty nutrition, spoiled food
Fur Damage	Hair loss (sometimes local), bald spots, dandruff, scabs	Skin disease from parasites (mites, lice) or fungus
Refusal to Eat	The rat eats little or nothing.	Illness, tooth problem, heatstroke
Loss of Balance	The rat is insecure on its feet, staggers, or falls over.	Inflammations or abscesses inside the ear; fungal infection, ear mites
Bloody urine	Bloody, strong-smelling urine, pain at urinating	Kidney or bladder infection
Holding Head at an Angle	The head is continually tipped at an angle.	Serious inner-ear infection
Scratching	The rat scratches at inflamed and scabby areas on the skin.	Serious itching of damaged skin from parasite infestation
Arched Back	Strongly arched sitting posture	General symptom of illness
Drooling	Excess saliva flow	Tooth problems, swallowed foreign object
Tumors	Palpable swellings under the skin or an enlarged abdomen, trouble breathing, poor appetite, pain	Abscesses, lipoma, infections, often cancerous growths
Restlessness	Hyperactive behavior, often accompanied by scratching and licking	Itching and skin problems from parasite infestation

A spoon for health: With illnesses that are caused by infectious agents, the sick animal must be separated from the rest to keep from spreading the problem. The sick rat is then treated in the second cage.

The Most Common Illnesses Among Rats

The sooner an illness is detected and treated, the greater the prospects for a cure. This is particularly true for rats, since illnesses in them can develop very quickly, which complicates treatment. Treating sick animals is the proper realm of the veterinarian; home treatment can prove fatal for the rodents. If you suspect an infectious disease, you should immediately consult with a veterinarian. Only a reliable diagnosis and immediate treatment can keep the other cage dwellers from becoming infected with the pathogen.

Respiratory Infections

Causes. Diseases of the respiratory passages can be caused by such things as bacteria and viruses. With rats the main cause of problems with the lungs and bronchi are drafts and excessively damp or dry air. Colds are thus not rare among the rodents. Even aggressive ammonia vapors, which build up relatively quickly in dirty cages, produce irritations, and eventually serious, lasting damage to the respiratory passages.

Symptoms. Rats that have caught cold sneeze, produce rattling or groaning noises when they breathe, exhibit shallow, rapid thoracic flank respiration, and often have a copious nasal discharge. Usually the entire organism is affected: the creatures are listless, scarcely eat, and lose weight; the fur becomes matted or thin. Bacterial respiratory infections weaken the immune defenses, which makes older rats in particular susceptible to serious diseases.

Treatment. For mild colds, heat (from a heat lamp); for serious infections, the veterinarian must prescribe antibiotics. Vitamins and minerals may build up the sick animal's immunity for recovery.

Skin Diseases

Causes. Many skin and fur problems are triggered by parasites and fungi. But allergies can also lead to stubborn skin

damage. *Bumblefoot* refers to a special set of symptoms that occur primarily in overweight male rats: They have a strong tendency to form stubborn abscesses on the balls of the hind feet.
Symptoms. Animals suffering from skin problems usually scratch and lick themselves endlessly to relieve themselves from the annoying itch caused by the inflamed and scabby areas. Skin ailments also damage the fur: They can lead to hair loss and typically local bald spots.

Rats with bumblefoot limp noticeably, for they cannot set down the infected, painful foot.
Treatment. An abscess on the ball of the foot must be treated immediately by a veterinarian to relieve the pain; keep the animal on clean, dry bedding. Diagnosis is often difficult with fungal and parasitic infestations, and treatment is almost always prolonged.

Mites, Lice, and Fleas

Causes. Increased incidence of parasites is generally a symptom of improper living conditions: uncleanness, faulty nutrition, neglected care, long-term conflicts in the pack, or stress from noise and continuous disturbances, plus much more. Newly acquired rats or other pets may be a source of external parasites.
Symptoms. Thin, matted fur, usually local hair loss; formation of scales and scabs, particularly noticeable on the ears. Back, sides, and face are particularly affected. The rats become restless and continually scratch or lick themselves.

MY PET

Too Thin or Too Fat?

When an animal loses weight quickly, it is a symptom of illness. Overweight, on the other hand, damages bones and joints and significantly reduces the rat's life expectancy. Check to see if your rodents are in the acceptable weight range.

The Test Begins:

○ Do the rat's bones protrude? Does this apply to several or all the animals?
○ Does the scale show that a rat has lost more than about an ounce (20 g) in a week?
○ Are some pack members more lethargic and less fond of climbing than the others?
○ Is there always food left over in the dishes, and do the rats hoard large stockpiles?
○ Are there any animals that keep getting thinner in spite of a good appetite?

My Test Results:

2 **Quarantine Box.** When disease is suspected, rats can be kept for a short time in a sick bay. Minimal accessories include a house, and food and water dishes.

1 **Fitness Check.** A healthy rat is cheerful and curious. Withdrawn, lethargic behavior is not infrequently the first sign of illness.

3 **Fur Problems?** Matted fur, scab formation, hair loss, pronounced restlessness, and continual scratching are typical symptoms of a parasite infection.

Mange mites and lice trigger similar symptoms; the lice can be detected with the naked eye. Fleas are rare on rodents. Treatment. Immediately consult a veterinarian if you encounter suspicious circumstances. Separate affected animals from the group to keep other animals from becoming infested.

Tapeworms and Roundworms

Causes. Tapeworms and roundworms are endoparasites that freeload inside the body of their host.
Symptoms. Especially with roundworms, a significant infestation interferes with the rat's health. The fur is matted, and the rat loses weight and acts lethargic. It may even result in intestinal blockage.
Treatment. Diagnosis and treatment by a veterinarian, generally requiring evaluation of a fecal sample.

Tumors

Causes. Especially with older animals, the formation of swellings is not uncommon in rats.
Symptoms. Tumors occur frequently on the abdomen and mammaries. You may notice a growth on or under the skin. With internal tumors, you may notice an enlarging abdomen or general symptoms related to organ dysfunction, including signs of pain, change in behavior, difficulty breathing, or reluctance to eat. Veterinarians can determine if growths are benign or malignant and can remove tumors.
Treatment. A small tumor that is detected early and has not metastasized usually can be removed successfully through surgery.

Stomach and Intestinal Ailments

Causes. Worm infestation, bacteria, non-worm parasites, gastrointestinal tumors, faulty nutrition, hairballs in the stomach, swallowed foreign object.

Symptoms. Worms (see facing page) and improper nutrition can trigger diarrhea and constipation; the animals frequently lose weight. Hairballs (bezoars) result when many hairs are swallowed during grooming; they clump together in the stomach and remain in place. As with foreign objects, this leads to constipation and refusal to eat.

Treatment. Have the veterinarian check for worms; surgical removal of large bezoars that cannot be eliminated. Preventive measures: Plastic and similar materials that can be gnawed and swallowed have no place inside the cage.

Discharge from Nose and Eyes

Causes. Parasite and bacterial infection, stress, general signs of indisposition and illness, inadequate living conditions.

Symptoms. Increased reddish secretion from the nose ("bloody nose") and the corners of the eyes. This involves a normally clear secretion formed by the Harderian glands and serves as a lubricant for moving the eyelids. At the start of an illness it turns red. Matted eyes are also a sign that a rat is feeling indisposed or an illness is beginning.

Treatment. In all cases the animal should be taken to a veterinarian to determine the true cause.

Ear Infections

Causes. Inflammations or abscesses in the middle or inner ear, plus infestation of mites and fungi.

Symptoms. An unpleasant odor from the ear is often the first symptom of an

CHECKLIST

Communicable Diseases

Zoonoses are infectious diseases that can be communicated to people from animals — and vice versa. The risk of infection from rats kept inside a house is very low. But you should still pay attention to good hygiene in dealing with animals.

○ Leptospirosis. An infectious disease transmitted by field mice and brown rats, among others. Pet rats can become infected if they are allowed to run free outdoors – then they can also infect humans. Symptoms in humans: usually similar to a cold, but also kidney problems and meningitis.

○ Salmonellosis. In an animal a salmonella infection can be latent and remain undiscovered. Meticulous cleanliness in dealing with animals is the surest protection against contracting an infection. Salmonellosis and leptospirosis must be reported to authorities.

○ Rat-Bite Fever and Sodoku Disease. Bacterial infections that are transmitted by bite and scratch wounds. Symptoms: fever, head pains, nausea, pains in muscles and joints. Both diseases are rare.

○ More common are colds and flus traveling from humans to rats, which are particularly susceptible to respiratory problems.

infection or a parasite infestation. Because an inner ear infection often involves the balance organ, afflicted animals are often unstable in their movements and stagger, fall over, or hold their head at an angle. Matting around the rim of the ear is typical for a mange mite infestation.

Treatment. A veterinarian is the only one who can provide a precise diagnosis; usually good results are obtained with antibiotics or treatment for mites.

Tooth Problems

Causes. Problems with the rodent teeth are a severe handicap to a rat. Usually the problem is excessive growth of the teeth, but abscesses and infections can contribute.

Symptoms. Difficulty in eating and drinking; with significant pain food intake will often cease altogether, and the creatures lose weight. Common secondary symptom: pronounced salivation.

Treatment. As a preventive measure, provide plenty of material to gnaw so that the teeth can be worn down. Regularly check the condition of the teeth,

especially with older animals. Excessively long rodent teeth must be shortened.

Wounds and Injuries

Causes. Bites in conflicts with other rats, broken legs and jaws as the result of falls, bruises (e.g., the tail), abrasions.

Symptoms. When bite wounds become infected and form abscesses, a rat visibly feels unwell and is in pain. Injuries to the tail (a break or a bruise) are even more painful. With a broken leg the injured member cannot support any weight or is pulled in.

Treatment. Wounds and injuries must be treated by a veterinarian—even apparently harmless bite wounds. A fall can result in internal injuries that can be detected only with a thorough examination.

Caring for Sick Rats

In case of illness the veterinarian is the right person to see. The following measures will help with the treatment:

▸ With infectious diseases, always keep the afflicted animal apart from the others.
▸ Pay attention to the correct room temperature and humidity; avoid draft at all costs.
▸ After consultation with the veterinarian, use a heat lamp, with care not to cause a burn.
▸ Use a disposable syringe without a needle or a dropper to dribble liquid medicines and nutrient solutions into the side of the mouth.
▸ Put a rat on a diet only on the advice of a veterinarian.

TIP

Administering Medicines Properly

Give medications only in accordance with the veterinarian's instructions, and at the same time every day. Tablets are mixed with semisolid food or ground up; drops are dribbled into the mouth. With antibiotics, usually no milk products should be given. Important: Use no drugs from human medicine.

Alternative Medicine

Natural healing processes such as homeopathy and Bach flower remedies are intended to activate the self-healing powers of the organism. They have proven their worth for a long time, even with animals. The veterinarian or a nonmedical practitioner decides when a treatment makes sense or promises success.

Homeopathy. Homeopathic preparations come in the form of drops, small balls, and powder. For treating rats, the little straw balls (globuli) are a good choice, for they are easy to administer and they taste good.

Bach Flower Remedies. The basis of the therapy developed by the English doctor Edward Bach is thirty-eight preparations that are produced from natural substances and used for behavior problems such as aggressiveness, stress, restlessness, and fear.

Even in close contact there is little risk of getting an infection from rats kept inside the house.

Are Rats a Health Risk?

The risk of getting an infection from a rat kept as a pet is very low. Instances of rat bite fever, the most significant disease transmissible from rats to humans (see page 91) are rare, and the infection can be combated effectively with antibiotics. In dealing with rats, the same thing applies as with other pets: Pay attention to diligent care and meticulous cleanliness (especially in the cage), and wash your hands after every contact. Explain to your children that rats do not belong in bed, and that they can be stroked, but not kissed.

Questions About
Care and Health

(?) Since I don't want to have to worry about my rats while I am on vacation, I have arranged to have an experienced pet sitter take care of them. What arrangements should we make in case something goes wrong or an animal becomes seriously ill during this time?

In case of doubtful circumstances, and in order to avoid misunderstandings or trouble between you and the caregiver later on, you should put the agreement about the vacation care into writing. This has nothing to do with mistrust, but is a protection for both sides. With rental contracts, generally form contracts are used to cover all the essentials and keep things clear. "Vacation Caregiver" contracts are designed quite similarly; you can find these on the Web pages of various clubs for rats and other pets and print them out (see the addresses on page 141).

(?) Our twins and their rats are bosom buddies and continually cuddle with one another. Can the children get sick from the animals?

The same standard used for all other pets also applies to rats: As long as the most important ground rules are observed, you needn't worry. Cuddling and hugging are permissible, but licking and kissing are not. Rats have no business in the children's bed, and of course hands need to be washed after every contact with the animals and after puttering around in the cage.

(?) Every day I check to make sure that my rats are eating well, behaving normally, and taking part in the life of the pack. Are these adequate precautionary measures for their health?

The daily health check is important; once a week you must also inspect your animals more thoroughly. This includes feeling over their body for knots and other swellings; an inspection of skin and coat for bald spots, hair loss, sores, and wounds (it's best to rub against the lay of the fur); checking the eyes, ears, rodent teeth (are they worn down enough?) and anal region. A weight check is also essential. If an animal has lost weight, in many cases it is an early sign of illness.

(?) It's easy to check if the rodent teeth are in good shape. But what about the molars? Are there no problems with them?

Unlike the rodent teeth, the molars do not keep growing and are subjected to less stress, so they rarely cause problems. Infections unfortunately often remain undetected for a long time, even to the point where the jaw is affected. Timely treatment by a veterinarian is particularly important in this case. If a rat refuses to eat and visibly loses weight, you should always think about the molars.

When I clip my rats' claws, they rarely sit still, and often pull back at the critical moment—and I have nipped a blood vessel. Is there no solution to this annoying problem?
If the claws get worn down enough in running and climbing, they rarely if ever need to be trimmed. A flat stone with a rough surface works well for this: Place it in a "high-density traffic" area in the cage. Coarse tightropes and climbing ropes (for example, made of sisal) also keep the claws short.

With sick and very old animals that don't get much exercise, though, you can't avoid trimming the claws. This is best done by two people: One person holds the foot and toes, and the second carefully applies the nail clippers or scissors.

One of my rats is an albino. She keeps swinging her head back and forth, and I have never seen this in her comrades. Is she sick, or is she suffering from a behavioral disturbance?
Neither. Albinos lack the pigmentation not only in the fur, but also in the eyes. They are red because the blood vessels in the back of the eye shine through. Red eyes are coupled with reduced visual acuity. To compensate for this, albinos move their head back and forth to focus better on objects. Their eyes are also very sensitive to light and must never be exposed to harsh light, such as spotlights.

Why do the rats eat only a few bites when they go to the food dish?
There are three reasons for this: First, a rat's stomach is naturally small and can take in only a small quantity of food. Second, there is rarely any jealousy about food in the pack, so nobody needs to eat quickly. And since the cage dwellers' food dish— in contrast to their wild relatives—is always amply stocked, nobody has to worry about food.

Should a sick rat always be segregated from the rest of the group?
Separate quarters are unavoidable in the case of a communicable disease, so that the other animals don't get infected. A separate cage also makes sense for sick and weak animals for which the veterinarian has prescribed a diet or that regularly need medicine.

Learning, Playing, and Keeping Busy

For rats, idleness is nearly as detrimental as the wrong food.
A cage in which they can go on journeys of discovery and romp to
their heart's desire is just what they need.

Acrobats, Explorers, and Diggers

Rats are curious about everything and everybody, continually on the go, and they get bored when there is nothing to do. The intelligent rodents remain fit and healthy only when they can regularly keep busy and get in lots of play.

FULL STEAM AHEAD Of course, rats also need to sleep. But when they are awake, things really happen: A healthy rat rarely sits still. It is always out and about, testing its fitness and physical mastery on the climbing rope and balancing. It burrows enthusiastically in the bedding and the digging box, curiously sticks its nose into every dark corner, and waits impatiently at the cage bars until the door opens and it is finally invited to take a stimulating reconnaissance tour in adventure land.

The Legacy from the Ancestors

For wild rats, mobility and bustling about, just like the characteristic curiosity, are not ends in themselves, but rather essentials of life and survival strategy. The rodents have many enemies and competitors. This requires the constant presence and alertness of the pack in checking and defending the territory. The same applies for the often fatiguing and demanding search for appropriate food sources and the often dangerous exploration of unknown terrain. This heritage remains unbroken in pet rats, even though they don't need to

continually delimit their territory or go in search of food. In addition, in tame rats a playful behavior is evident that is less noticeable in their wild relatives. And it is rather rare in the animal world, for the enjoyment of play does not end with adulthood.

Intelligence Required

When you look into the dark button eyes of a rat, you often have the impression that nothing can get by it—and this has nothing to do with visual acuity. And rats often enough prove that this supposition is quite close to reality by

Pot peepers: ▶
The dark interior
of a clay pot is
explored tho-
roughly. It's also
a great place to
hide and watch
everything
without being
seen.

The main thing is that something is happening.

▶ **1** **Spa Cure.** Nearly all rats love water. A foot bath in a bathtub goes well with washing the entire body (right).

▶ **2** **Balancing Act.** The balancing movements with the tail keep the run across the twig from ending in a fall (middle).

▶ **3** **On the Right Track.** Toys made of solid natural wood are sturdy, and free of pigments, toxins, and sharp corners and edges (far right).

performing tricky tasks. In so doing the rodents rely on both the ability to store up the facts of an area and their tremendous sense of direction. This is what makes them the champions of the maze.

Playtime

In order to have fun you have to have all your senses engaged. Invite the cage clan to play during their activity phases in the morning and the evening. A sensitive rat person never disturbs the animals when they are eating or grooming themselves, or during the siesta. But for many rats that carry their human securely in their heart, the joint play and cuddling time is much more important than their nap, and they eagerly crawl out of the sleeping houses as soon as the person comes into the room.

Hide-and-Seek

Dark corners, hidey-holes, caves, and tunnels have a magical attraction for rats. They provide security and protection; from inside, they can keep the surroundings in view without being seen. And maybe they will even find something edible.

Everything that makes rats curious and into which they can stick their nose is appropriate for games of hide-and-seek: boxes, cartons, bags, and cardboard or clay pipes. You don't need to talk your rodents into it: A small treat placed at the goal is adequate incentive. Just try it when the rats are outside the cage; inside their cage the rats know all the corners and crannies and will quickly discover even difficult hiding places. A search outside the cage requires more brains. It's best to try it first with two or three animals so you don't have to search for parolees that turn up missing.

▶ Place a treat in an open box high enough so that the rat can look over the edge when it sits up on its hind legs.

▶ Place three dissimilar open boxes next to one another. There is a treat inside

only one of them (see the color test on page 20).

▸ Repeat the foregoing test. But after the first successful runs, change the position of the boxes.

▸ Hide treats between the layers of paper in the digging box. Then several players can search at the same time.

▸ A tower with several floors provides long-term fun and lots of skylights and holes to crawl through. Here too you can send the rodents on a tidbit safari.

▸ There are also stimulating search games in mazes made from individual sections that can be put together in new labyrinth patterns (see page 104).

The Right Training for Steeplejacks

Even though pet rats are descended from primarily ground-dwelling brown rats, they are still gifted and enthusiastic climbers. But because even climbing

geniuses sometimes miss the mark, hammocks and nets must provide protection in places where a major fall is possible.

A Climbing Tree for All Seasons. In many cages the climbing tree is the center of rat life and the multipurpose device of a thousand possibilities—with perches, sleeping houses, climbing and side ropes, plus connections to all the

TIP

Limited Edition

Give your rats specific playground apparatuses and toys only for a limited time or while they are outside the cage. This can be a new tunnel system, a climbing tower set up in a different way, or simply a different ball. The limited entertainment nearly always provides for total enthusiasm.

EXTRA FEATURE FOR PARENTS

Rules of Play Preserve Friendship

Rats are almost always ready for all kinds of fun and adventure, and quickly discover their love for children who spend a lot of time with them and deal with them lovingly. And if both sides observe the most important rules for play, a long-term friendship can result.

PLAYMATES WITH CLEVERNESS AND INTELLI-GENCE For children playing is life. Through play they discover their world, their talents, and their preferences. Children need play-things. But how can anything compare with lively, clever playmates that accompany them on their journeys of discovery, contin-ually stimulate their imaginations with new things, amaze them, and make them laugh?

Respecting Needs

Toys can be handled dispassionately and put into a corner when the game ceases to be fun. You have to be considerate of playmates, though—particularly of small, sensitive four-legged creatures. An under-standing for the animals' needs is a pre-requisite for permission to play with them.

Understanding Behavior

Playmates must understand one another and know what the other wants. Does the other feel like playing, or rather prefer to go a different way? Is the partner uncertain or even fearful? It is the parents' duty to explain to their children the rats' most important reactions and behaviors and show them the proper way to deal with the rodents (see page 56).

Earning Trust

Rats have a big heart. They are open to relationships and always curious about new things. It is not difficult to win their trust. But one must not disappoint them, for it is hard for them to forget a broken confidence.

Playing by the Rules

Here's how to keep playing fun for children and rats:
> Don't invite rats to play when they are sleepy or in the process of eating.
> Play in familiar surroundings and only with two or three animals at the same time.
> Choose simple games (playing with balls, hiding small objects, e.g., in the digging box), climbing, and balancing (place food at the goal).

Secure the playground in advance with nets or hammocks to prevent falls.
> Game Over: Goals for play are only a stim-ulus and need not be achieved. Take a break or end the game if the rodents don't feel like continuing or if they become tired. Young and older rats in particular should be encouraged to play only for a short time.
> Eyes Open: Keep a particularly sharp eye on the floor during play so nobody acciden-tally steps on an animal.

stories. Sisal or hemp ropes wrapped around the trunk make it easier for old-timers to climb up and down. An eating bowl on a platform stays clean longer than one on the ground floor. An outer branch is the best place to take refuge from the hectic group life. Important: a solid stand and secure attachment.

Aerial Training with Rope and Ladder. Often there is a lot of traffic in both directions on the climbing rope. Rodents do gymnastics and climb with astonishing skill on a stout rope that provides purchase for the claws (and simultaneously wears them down).

The thick knots in the rope afford the less athletic users a pause to catch their breath. A rope stretched tight and secured top and bottom makes it easy to reach even the upper floors. Athletic characters prefer free-hanging ropes— they may get a special kick out of the pendulum motion, as with a swing.

Test Track for Balancing Artists. Rats have a highly developed sense of balance and test it at every opportunity. So side ropes must be well secured and must not be too thin. Many tightrope walkers overestimate their abilities. In that case it is good to have a net to break the freefall.

2 **A Flower for the Best.** Most mazes are an easy exercise for rats. They get the hang of it by at least the second or third test run. It's great when there is a tasty greeting waiting at the exit.

▼

▲

1 **Simply Divine.** In this house with many doors there is something different in every room for the precocious visitors to discover and sniff. This really is an ideal second house.

2 **Keyboarding Help.** A rat must stick its inquisitive nose anyplace something moves or makes strange noises, whether it's a computer mouse or a keyboard.

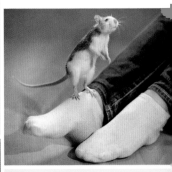

1 **An Invitation to Go Out and Play.** The open cage door is something no rat can resist when there is so much to discover outside.

3 **Facing the Climb.** A favorite person is the first choice for a climbing tree. This also calls for some cuddling.

A Workplace for Diggers

Anyplace where it is possible to dig, rats are filled with enthusiasm. This works in the bedding, but it's much nicer in their own digging box. You can fill it with shredded newspaper or toilet paper, or with leaves, hay, or loose sand. In the enthusiasm of the encounter, the filling often gets spread over the surroundings. You can get your excavating crew into high gear by hiding little treats in the box.

Splashing and Bathing

Rats have no fear of water, and they are excellent swimmers and divers. But since every rat has its own preferences, in addition to genuine water rats there are also sticks in the mud that don't like to get wet. So let your animals decide who wants to bathe and who does not.

▸ Tub no. 1: A wading pool with shallow water. The rats must be able to stand securely in it. Put in a ladder or a ramp for climbing out.

▸ Tub no. 2: A larger and higher container with a water depth of approximately 6 inches (15 cm), for diving fans. Provide a small area for sitting and a way to climb out.

▸ Bathing takes place only outside the cage, for otherwise the bedding will get wet.

▸ Slices of cucumber or carrot in the water increase the fun and can convert even the fuddy-duddies.

▸ Dry the rats after bathing and make sure they are not exposed to draft.

Crazy for the Maze

Wild brown rats make their way in dark cellars, sewer systems full of twists and turns, dumps, and demolished houses. In the maze their descendants show that they too possess an unerring sense of direction.

Training for Beginners and Pros

Start the test series with a simple maze, and increase the difficulty as soon as the players head for the reward without wrong turns. Rats orient themselves with scent markings. Clean the passageways between attempts to keep subsequent test runs from becoming too easy.

▸ A maze for beginners: A simple passageway with only one fork (a Y-maze). The reward is placed at the end of one branch.
▸ Intelligence required: A system of passageways with several branches and dead ends. Reward at the exit.
▸ Pros on tour: A complex maze with lots of branches, dead ends, bridges, hurdles, stairs, tunnels, with rotary traffic, and a central square from which several roads originate. Reward in the center.
▸ False Trail: Put the reward in a dead end.

With tunnels, tubes, and underpasses, be mindful of the smallest diameter so that stoutly built animals don't get stuck inside. Provide long pipes with several exit holes. And remember, rats usually explore strange terrain in twos or threes. Several animals may go on tour in a large maze.

Playthings to Avoid

Rats can get hurt with these playthings or inappropriate materials.

○ Wire mesh running wheels: There is a high danger that legs, feet, or tail will get caught or crushed in the open mesh.

○ Plastic running balls: Running inside the ball puts a lot of strain on the back and bends it too far outward; in addition there is insufficient air exchange.

○ Soft plastic: If it gets chewed, it can block the air pipe when it gets swallowed, and lead to suffocation.

○ Hamster fluff and household cotton: The toes' claws get caught in the cotton; high risk of injury.

○ Perches with a wire core: There is a risk of injury if the perch gets chewed and the wire is exposed.

○ Wire mesh food balls: A rat can injure a leg when it tries to get to the food (with metal and plastic models).

○ Balls of wool: Claws get caught.

○ Plastic running tubes: There is no traction for the feet inside the smooth tubes.

○ Toys made of evergreen woods: These are inappropriate for rats, for they contain lots of resin.

MY PET

Who's the Best in the Maze?

Rats can't be beat at orienteering. But who is the champion of champions? For this test you need a simple and a more demanding maze, a couple of treats as rewards, and a stopwatch.

The Test Begins:

○ Simple Y-maze with one branch. The reward is placed at the exit from one branch. Which rat completes three successful runs in a row?

○ Y-maze with an open and a closed branch. Food in the closed branch. Who is the fastest at finding the reward and then the exit (stopwatch)?

○ Large maze: Like the second attempt, but here the reward is in the center. Stop the clock.

My Test Results:

A Homemade Maze

Even if you aren't skilled at working with your hands, you can build a rat maze yourself and make it fit your notions in size and layout.

▶ Material: The right choices are wood and plastic; passageways made of cardboard need frequent replacement.

▶ Keeping it clean: All components of the system should at least be wiped with a damp cloth, and parts installed in the cage must be easily accessible.

▶ Always something new: A modular system of units that can easily be taken apart and put back together in numerous variations is always better than a fixed maze. This provides for lasting stimulation in play.

▶ 3-D system: Rats always like to climb. A maze that goes up and down, perhaps over several stories, guarantees the animals will have fun. New elements include stairs, ramps, chimneys, and climbing tubes at an angle (both with aids for climbing in).

▶ Inappropriate: Do not use hamster tunnels—the smooth surfaces provide no traction for feet and claws in climbing.

▶ Use no glues with solvents that give off harsh substances and could harm the animals' breathing passages.

▶ If you don't like to tinker: You can find ready-made models in pet shops and on the Internet. Look for sturdy construction with no sharp edges.

Fun for Playful Rogues

With these tests you can find out if your cheeky rodent can use its brains as well as its fitness and skill.

▶ Bowl Test: A treat is placed beneath a lightweight bowl made of translucent plastic (with the bowl upside down). The rat can see the treat, but can get it only when it tips over the bowl. A small piece of wood under the edge of the bowl will create a space into which the rat can push a paw.

▶ Crack the Egg: A hard-boiled egg resists the rodent teeth. Does it occur to your rat to roll the egg to an elevated location and push it downhill to break open the shell?

▶ Fishing in a Box: Place a tempting treat inside a closed cardboard box with several small holes. Which playmate is the first to gnaw on a hole until it can reach in with one paw, or even climb into the box?

Back into the Cage

For the cage residents the time spent running around outside the cage is the high point of the day. These play possibilities will keep them enthused:

▶ Mobile Climbing Paradise: A sturdily anchored climbing tree with houses, platforms, climbing ropes, and a swing. The final detail is the treats hanging on the tree.

▶ Fitness Center: A rat tower with observation platforms and lots of entry and exit holes. The meandering route from floor to floor requires lots of skill. The rats can take a siesta inside.

▶ Labyrinth: There is plenty of space in the room for a large, complex maze.

The only thing is that you have to take everything apart after the rats return to their cage.

▶ Journey to the Unknown: Journeys of discovery on bookshelves and cabinets only with your supervision.

▶ Back to the Cage: When the rats are free, the cage door remains open so that they can return on their own. Stairs or a ladder will make it easier for them to get in. At first a treat will make sure that going home is a positive experience.

This Multi-tenant residence has observation platforms, several stories, and a large ramp.

▼

▸ Outwitting Deserters: Lure a missing rat out of its hiding place with a treat and let it climb onto your open hand. If the rat doesn't cooperate, hold a short cardboard or clay pipe in front of its nose and help with a gentle push on the rear end in case it doesn't crawl in voluntarily. Never grab a rat by the scruff of the neck or the tail.

A Running Wheel for Rats?

Most of the running wheels available on the market are inappropriate for rats: The diameter of the wheel is almost always so small that when running, the rat's back is very arched and under too much stress. All open mesh constructions are terribly dangerous, because legs and tail can get stuck in them and get broken or crushed. A running wheel for rats must be used to satisfy these requirements: a very large diameter

DID YOU KNOW THAT . . .

. . . big jumps are risky for rats?

Rats are active in the dusk and at night. Visual acuity is less important at those times. Because the rodents also have only very limited spatial vision, they can't see distant objects clearly and judge distances imprecisely. Long jumps can lead to nasty falls. So when you set up the cage, make sure that the resident go-getters are not tempted to make excessively long jumps.

No Fighting over Toys

Two water bottles, two food dishes, and several houses are requirements in the rat cage. With four or more residents, too, the favorite toys should be provided in pairs. The main object of desire is the swing, which is also used as a hammock by many of the little snoozers. A second swing avoids trouble and gives even the weaker ones a chance at unbridled play fun.

(14–16 inches/35–40 cm), a completely enclosed running surface (for example, of wood) to protect against leg injuries, and smooth and easy running on maintenance-free ball bearings.

The size of the running barrel inevitably requires larger outside dimensions. Only in rare cases does the cage offer enough room for a giant wheel of this type. As a fitness offering, it can be placed anyplace you want when the rats are outside the cage—even if not all rats are such dedicated running-wheel enthusiasts as Golden Hamsters, for example.

Rats know what is good for them and that
play keeps body and soul together—
true to the motto that only an active rat is a healthy rat.

The Stuff of Which Good Playthings Are Made

The following are the right materials for apparatuses for play and gymnastics:
Wood. Wood must not be treated, covered with plastic film, or waterproof, and must be finished with nontoxic varnish. Brush off untreated wood regularly under hot water or vinegar and water.
Plastic. Hard plastic and Plexiglas are easy to keep clean. Smooth plastic is not appropriate as a running surface. Soft plastic can get gnawed and swallowed, with a danger of getting stuck in the rat's throat.
Cork. A very lightweight material; objects installed in the cage must be well anchored or weighted down. Untreated cork can be gnawed without danger.
Stone. Natural stones, cellular concrete, and cinder block are good running surfaces. The rough surface of the stone provides traction for the claws and simultaneously wears them down.
Ceramic. Clay and ceramic pipes, which are good choices for the rat cage, are available in every hardware store. The heavy material must be attached securely.
Corrugated Cardboard. Tunnels, houses, runways, and ramps can be made from card stock and corrugated cardboard in the twinkling of an eye. Disadvantage: Cardboard quickly soaks up moisture and urine and must be replaced at frequent intervals.

Paper. Paper tissues, newspaper, and toilet paper are appropriate for the digging box, for houses, and for wrapping up "surprises."
Sand. Bird sand and dirt are the right stuff for rodents bitten by the digging bug. It's best to offer this only outside the cage.
Textiles. Linen, cotton, and denim are ideal for hammocks and swings. Wash new textiles to remove the sizing (an applied petroleum-based chemical). Careful: Because of the loops in the weave, terry cloth is a foot trap in which toes and claws can easily get caught.

Everything That Moves

As long as it rolls or bounces, rats are right on the ball. Rubber, plastic, and

Where's it happening? A healthy rat is always active and loves sports and games.
▼

wooden balls, nuts, spools, and dice are ideal. Avoid mesh balls and balls of wool.

More Play Fun

Whenever there is something to experience, rats are there right away; they are not afraid of unaccustomed challenges, and are enthusiastic about every type of game—especially when their owner takes part.

Hurdle Training for Top Athletes

Sprinting over the hurdles poses no problem for a quick, confident rodent. At first, start with two or three hurdles a little over an inch high (3–4 cm). Set up the track so that the rats can't run under or around the hurdles (for example, with cardboard walls along the sides). A treat waits at the finish line. With time, increase the distance and put in more and higher hurdles. For advanced hurdlers use a combination run over hurdles and through pipes or underpasses.

Freestyle Wrestling

Many rats like to cuddle with a human. Nudge your playmate with a finger, turn its hind end to one side, or drum gently (!) with your fingers on its stomach. Soft, gentle sounds reinforce the playful character. It will play along and defend itself. Take a break or end the game if it becomes too rowdy and wild, or the rat uses its teeth. Always play with just one animal. Important: This game is absolutely taboo for children.

A Sightseeing Tour

There is nothing more exciting for rats than a big world to discover. And it's best on the human's shoulder or in the shirt pocket. But only absolutely hand-tame animals may go on tour, and even then the excursion must be restricted to familiar and secure terrain. Never take a rat shopping or for a stroll through town. Even calm dispositions can experience panic in unforeseen situations, fall down, and get hurt—or even run away. In addition, a confrontation with a person who is afraid of or disgusted by rats fans the flames of old prejudices and is hardly calculated to improve the rodents' image.

Cuddle Time

For most rats the petting time with the trusted human is pure bliss. But there are individual differences. Many cuddlers can become so insistent that you can scarcely keep them off your body. Others find cuddling dumb and prefer to keep their distance.

A Heart for Old-Timers

With older animals, mobility and strength decline; they move with less assurance and get out of breath more quickly.

- Ramps with treads across them provide traction for the claws and make it easier for old and weak animals to climb up. Wide stairs with a coating and railings that provide a grip are good for seniors.
- The animals can take a break on the knots in the climbing ropes.
- They can climb up on strength-saving ladders at a shallow angle.
- Safety nets under runways and cross ropes prevent falls.
- Additional houses and resting places provide protection from wild youths.

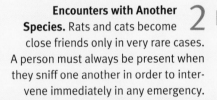

1 **Lookout Platform.** The parolees have the best view from the top floor of the cat scratching tree. A net under the platform protects the acrobats from a fall.

2 **Encounters with Another Species.** Rats and cats become close friends only in very rare cases. A person must always be present when they sniff one another in order to intervene immediately in any emergency.

3 **Inspection Tour.** What could be better than exploring the whole house? But uncontrolled exercise quickly creates problems for the owner when the parolee is no longer anywhere to be seen.

4 **A Dream Home.** Their own home in a drawer filled with delightfully soft clothes. And far and wide, no other rats to compete for the pleasure. Anyone who leaves here voluntarily has nobody to blame but themselves.

Questions About
Play and Activities

? Our three rascals scoot through the maze at top speed and snap up the reward. How can I make the game more interesting?

If nothing inside the maze changes, the orienteering experts have an easy time of it. Set up the whole maze in a mirror image. Everything that was on the right side moves to the left, and vice versa. Of course this makes sense only with a complex setup, not with simple Y-shapes. Variation no. 2: The rats are distracted by an intense smell (such as cheese). The source of the smell is outside the maze and exactly opposite from the finish and the reward.

? My rats love the seesaw. How can it be so dangerous?

Not all seesaws pose a risk. In models with a low fulcrum there is little danger of injury. But the situation is very different with high seesaws in which the board swings up high and then slams into the floor with lots of momentum. If a rat has a leg or a tail under the board at this instant, it may crush or break something.

? For our female rats, playing means taking every movable object into a hiding place. How can I break them of this?

Putting aside supplies is an inherited behavior; one never knows if there will be anything to eat tomorrow. As a result, they also hide toys that can be gnawed. Encourage the drive to play using rubber and plastic balls that rarely get dragged around; large balls cannot be seized with the teeth, but they are great for nudging and rolling. In addition, put off ball games until the rats are outside the cage and the storehouse is far away.

? There is a large play tower made of wood in the room for the rats to use when they are outside the cage, but the rats are interested only in the bookshelves and the chest of drawers. What's so exciting about them?

Why should things be any different with rats than with us? The grass is always greener on the other side of the fence. The play tower surely is exciting to the rats. But if they explore it every day, it soon holds no further mysteries for them. How much more stimulating a bookshelf is—it inspires the rats to climb and has not yet been explored. In next to no time you can give your play tower a new appeal: Line the floors with soft material, and hang pieces of cloth in the tower windows, because rats like to be in half-light. Make the whole team get a move on with food-search games in and around the tower.

? I keep reading that it's best to play with one's rats in the evening. Why? My two females are also wide awake and lively during the day.

Tips on keeping animals in handbooks and animal

magazines are always best on normal behaviors that can be expected. And with rats, which are active in the dusk and during the night, this means that they are particularly lively and active in the evening. But because rats can quickly adapt to altered living conditions, nowadays they take many of their cues for the daily routine from humans: They are almost always ready for playing a little game together. For people who work during the day it is good to know that your buddies will be wide awake when you get home in the evening. But whenever you want to play with the rodents, if you pull them out of sleep, you will not make any friends.

? **My rats cannot get enough bathing.** Two of them let themselves get dried off afterward, but one resists with all its strength. I want to keep it from catching cold. What should I do?

It is a show of trust when your rats give in to the procedure with the towel. But not every rat is ready for that, and you must not force the issue. After the bathing session, make sure that the rat can care for its fur in a warm location protected from draft, perhaps under a heat lamp (not too close). Also make sure that the bathing water is lukewarm.

? **One rat doesn't want to come out** and stays behind in the cage. It is not sick. What makes it do this?

There can be a variety of reasons for this: A new or shy animal is afraid of the strange surroundings; the cage gives it security. Older rats often avoid the physical exertion and prefer to take a nap during this time. Perhaps the rat also doesn't get along so well with the others and is happy to be alone for a while; in this case you should do some research into the cause. Finally, it may also be that on some previous excursions outside the cage the rat had an unpleasant experience.

? **I have one really affectionate rat that** always lets me carry it around and doesn't want to be in the cage. What should I do with it?

Cuddle monsters that unmistakably show their affection are not rare among rats. And it is much more exciting to be on a walking climbing tree than inside a cage. Cut back on the loving a little by taking the cuddly rat out of the cage only at specific times.

Reproduction and Rearing

Sexual maturity at eight weeks, six to eight litters per year, and six, ten, or more young per litter: With their reproduction strategy, rats have colonized every corner of the earth.

Mating Behavior and Pregnancy

Female rats are capable of conceiving every four to six days, and mate with several males. There is therefore a good chance that there will be offspring. The young are born after three weeks, nearly always without problems.

LOVE AND CARE A mother rat takes self-sacrificing care of her young ones, bundles everyone off to a calm place when there is not too much noise and bustle, and in serious cases defends them like a lioness. The care is necessary, for the young are born totally helpless: Newborn rats are typical altricial animals; they are naked, blind, and deaf, and perceive only touch, warmth, and smells. But they quickly graduate from the nursery (see page 120) and can even mate as early as seven to eight weeks old.

would lead to a dramatic overpopulation. Even if raising rats is charming and the various colorations (see pp. 24–29) are especially attractive, you should breed rats only if you have commitments from rat purchasers before you begin. Undesired reproduction occurs often enough through inattention on the part of the owner. Without purchasers these young animals will end up in an animal shelter or will simply be let go. It is irresponsible to consciously take this risk in breeding rats.

Precocious and Prolific

Sexual maturity in female rats living in the wild is reached at seven to eight weeks, and often a bit earlier in domesticated rats, and they are receptive to mating for twenty hours at a time on a cycle of four to six days. With an average litter size of eight young (but also up to twenty), the offspring from one mating pair of rats can add up to eight hundred children and grandchildren in a year. In the wild only a small number of the young animals have a chance of survival. With rodents living under the care of humans, unrestricted reproduction

It is easiest to avoid reproduction by owning animals of just one sex, such as a group of only females. ▶

113

Courtship and Mating

▶ **1** **Foreplay.** If the female rat is not ready to mate, it keeps running away from the male (right).

▶ **2** **Sniff Test.** The male rat is a polite suitor and behaves very considerately with his chosen bride (middle).

▶ **3** **Quick Action.** Mounting and copulation take just a few seconds, but the mating is repeated several times (far right).

Too Young to Bear Children

Female rats are capable of reproduction at seven to eight weeks—even though they are not fully grown and are still children. They are often overwhelmed by motherhood and raising the young, or don't know what to do with the off-spring. At the age of ten to twelve weeks they are capable of raising young. To avoid risks to the mother and the young, it is still better to wait until the sixth month.

The Unexpected Always Happens

Undesired reproduction often takes place more quickly than we would like:
▶ when females are kept with unneutered males;
▶ when female and male young rats are not separated early enough (prefer-ably after the fourth week);
▶ when you unsuspectingly buy a preg-nant female.

Courtship Display and Mating

Females in heat signal their receptive-ness to mating by emitting pheromones that are detected by the males in the pack and cause them to begin courtship.

The Suitor Gives Chase

Part of the ritual of foreplay involves the pursuit of the chosen female by the male; at first she keeps avoiding him and runs a short distance, but then stands still to make sure that he is fol-lowing her. Everything proceeds politely, without a tussle. Finally, both sniff each other in the genital region, and the female stands still and is ready to mate.

A Matter of Seconds

The typical posture is for the receptive female to present her hind part with straightened back and to move her tail to the side; the male mounts her. The mating itself takes no longer than a

couple of seconds, and is repeated several times in the following hours: A male rat can mount repeatedly during this time, but ejaculates sperm only on every tenth to fifteenth copulation. He grooms himself after every mating, but the female grooms only when she is impregnated. If the female is no longer receptive, a vaginal plug forms that prevents further copulation. During mating, both animals emit sounds that are not perceptible to humans. They signal their receptiveness to mating and may be intended to soothe the other males in the pack.

Playful Mounting

Males or females will even mount others of their own sex, as can be observed in young animals. As with other animals, this may be an expression of dominant behavior. The frequent role change is noteworthy, and it underscores the playful character of this same-sex mounting.

Pregnancy

The gestation period of rats is twenty to twenty-four days. Pregnancy uses up strength: The future mother needs high-quality, energy-rich food. She puts on weight, and her teats swell.

Unnoticed Pregnancy. Even a few days before giving birth, many pregnant females show neither clear physical nor behavioral changes. The typical nesting

TIP

Playing It Safe

The surest way to prevent unwanted offspring is to keep groups all of the same sex. The ideal choice is an all-female pack. In a mixed group the males must be neutered. Note: Even after neutering the males are potent for weeks (see page 116).

behavior also frequently occurs very late. When you buy animals of unknown origin, there is always a risk of bringing a pregnant female into the house.

A Place for the Nest. For the birthing place the female looks for a calm, fairly dim corner of the cage. Soft paper (paper towel) is a good choice for bedding. In this phase you should do as little as possible around the cage, for

Everything the Same. During pregnancy, the female should remain in the familiar cage and in her group. A transfer to her own lying-in bed would be very unsettling to the future mother. Her female friends from the pack often help with raising the young ones later on ("aunting behavior").

More Power to Mom. The food ration for the pregnant female is nearly doubled.

DID YOU KNOW THAT . . .

. . . male rats are still potent after being neutered?

Neutering a rat always involves risk. The operation should be considered only if it is unavoidable—as in the case of severe aggressiveness in a male. Otherwise keeping the sexes segregated is the simplest and surest way to prevent reproduction. But when a male rat must be neutered, this must be done no sooner than three months, and no later than eighteen months with older animals. In no case should the male be placed in with females right after the operation, for neutered animals remain potent for three to six weeks. After the operation, the male should be given additional vitamins and minerals. Spaying a female is even more costly than neutering a male. A veterinarian will decide on these measures only in case of health problems (such as sepsis of the uterus).

---

the future mother will start to build a nest in some other place if the previously selected place becomes too unsettled. Some females now act noticeably more distant from humans, but others seek their presence more actively.

She needs high-energy foods containing carbohydrates, additional vitamins and minerals, and more animal protein. Nursing mother rats have a much higher energy requirement during this time.

Birth and Rearing

The birth and the nursery are a strenuous full-time job for the mother. Still, she cares for all of her children persistently and lovingly until they are big enough to take care of themselves.

MOTHERS OF 100 CHILDREN
In the course of her life a female rat can have up to fifteen litters. With an average of eight babies per litter, that means more than a hundred offspring for one mother. But breeders stop using animals that have already given birth six or seven times. Female rats that are six to twelve months old give birth to the most viable and the largest litters. At this age there are also few birthing problems.

The Arrival of the Young

It is not always easy to detect when the birthing begins. Many animals become very restless, but others behave almost normally. Immediately before the delivery the female often licks her teats, genitalia, and stomach.

▶ Baby rats are usually born at night, and sometimes early in the morning.

▶ Depending on the number of babies, a normal birth lasts between twenty minutes and an hour. If it takes significantly longer, or if there are long breaks between individual births, things are not going right. Oftentimes the mother is simply so weak that immediate help from a veterinarian is required. The veterinarian should be alerted in advance in case there is a problem with birthing.

▶ There can be major differences in the size of litters. On the average eight young are born, but there are also litters with only four, and some with nearly twenty.

▶ During the first seven days the mother and babies should be left in peace as much as possible. You can take a quick look at the newborns when the new mother leaves the nest. But don't touch the little ones.

Female rats are good mothers that take care of their offspring tirelessly.

117

▲

The mother sets the good example: Her young ones like the same things she likes.

Mother with a Full-time Job

In the first three weeks the mother rat is on duty around the clock. She must nurse the young and keep them warm, pull back the babies that crawl off, and keep massaging their tummies with her tongue to stimulate digestion. She leaves the nest only to get a bit to eat for herself, drink a swallow, and do her business.

Helpless Babies. As typical altricial animals, the tiny newborns, which weigh only a few grams, are completely dependent on the mother's help: They are naked, blind, and deaf, and react only to warmth, touch, and smell. Constant physical contact with the mother and siblings is vitally important to them; otherwise the only thing that counts in this time is the teats that dispense food.

Energetic Aunts. Sometimes the female gets support in her strenuous job from the other grown females in the group: the "aunts" take loving care of the litter when the mother is not there.

Got Milk. Warmth and smell show the babies the arduous route to the mother's milk bar. During the three-week nursing time, each young animal prefers a specific teat. The strongest youngsters thus get the hindmost and the most productive among the total of eight pairs of teats.

Alarm Signal. If a young one gets lost, it calls loudly for the mother, who immediately reacts to the peeping. The rapid aid is necessary: A baby without physical contact with its siblings will cool down quickly. Because the thermoregulation does not yet work fully, the organism cannot yet keep the body temperature constant. Even other adult members of the pack carry back babies that have fallen out of the nest.

A Change of Address. The mother defends her young from all comers and usually reacts quite indignantly to all disturbances. If the nesting place no longer appears secure, she will even move with the babies. She takes each baby in her mouth and carries it to the new quarters. In transport the baby falls into a limp posture that protects it from injuries and facilitates the move for the mother.

Capable of Conception. Immediately after giving birth, the female is again capable of conceiving, but this is not encouraged due to the tremendous physical toll it would take so soon after delivery. This postpartum estrus lasts around twenty-eight hours. The biological reason for this is to ensure reproduction in case there are problems or stillborn young in the first litter.

Baby Rats
at a Glance

Naked and Helpless ▶

Newborn rats are naked and blind and completely dependent on the mother's help (right). Physical contact with one another provides warmth and security (far right).

◀ Discovering the World

The litter nest is still the absolute focus of the youngsters' world (far left). But the young rats develop quickly and soon begin their first excursions to discover the exciting new world (left).

Strength in Numbers ▶

Young rats do everything together. They feel secure and strong only in the company of their siblings (right). A sign of trust: the first treat from the hand of a human (far right).

◀ *Bonding through smell:
This tiny, inquisitive rat
is still totally helpless.
But because its sense of
smell is well developed, it
can grow accustomed to
the scent of humans even
at this tender age.*

A Quick Tour Through the Nursery

▸ At birth the babies weigh .17 to .21 ounce (5–6 g). After two weeks they are up to .7 ounce (20 g), after a month 2.1 to 2.8 ounces (60–80 g); in the second month they weigh up to 6.3 ounces (180 g), and in the third, a maximum of 9 ounces (260 g).

▸ Hair begins to grow on the second day of life; the markings on the fur can be seen as soon as the third day, and at sixteen days it is fully developed.

▸ The rodent teeth (incisors) break through between the eighth and tenth day; the ears open after the twelfth day, and two to four days later the eyes open.

▸ The babies play with one another starting with the third week; from around the twenty-second day on they begin their first excursions.

▸ After three to four weeks they are nearly weaned from the mother's milk and can take in solid food.

▸ At eight weeks, sometimes even earlier, rats are sexually mature. Females and males should be separated after the fourth week, but keep each sex together as a group.

▸ At six to seven weeks the young are independent. At the end of the fifth month the growth phase for the young is complete.

▸ Rats should not be used for breeding until they are six months old.

Determining the Sex of Young Rats

Here is how to identify the sex of young rats:

▸ Babies up to the fifth week: The distance from the penis to the anus is greater in males than the distance between the sex orifice and outlet of the urethra to the anus in female animals. The six pairs of teats are already visible in very young females.

▸ Starting with the fifth week: Males can easily be distinguished by the testicles that have moved from the abdominal cavity to the scrotum.

The First Step Toward Trust

The mother and babies stay together during the first days. In the second week you may gently stroke the young ones and pick them up—provided that the mother has no objections. That way you can check the physical makeup of the animals. Early contact with the babies is a significant first step in getting them used to the presence of humans. As soon as you can tell the boys from the girls, you should mark the sexes at the base of the tail with a swab and food coloring, especially in the case of large litters. That way they can be differentiated at a glance.

Boundless Play

Young rats are very active, and no later than the third week of life it becomes hard to keep them under control. The littermates test their abilities and fitness in wild games of chase and combat. Unfortunately, they don't always know their limits, and they endanger one another. It can happen that a half-grown rat you are holding on your hand suddenly decides to take a leap. To keep the impetuous youngsters from getting out of the cage, the inside of the bars need to be secured with wire screen. It would be easy for the nimble pipsqueaks to squeeze through the regular cage bars.

MY PET

A Personality Test for Junior Staff Members

Differences in disposition become evident in rats as early as childhood. Using simple experiments you can find out which of the young ones has what it takes to be boss and which are more reserved.

The Test Begins:
- Put a new house containing a tempting treat inside the cage (put older animals somewhere else in advance). Which youngster is the first to dare to enter the strange hut?
- Who tries out a new swing, and who merely observes the goings-on from a distance?
- Put an unfamiliar Y-maze into the room and place a reward at the end of one branch. Which young rat gets it most quickly? (Use a stopwatch.)

My Test Results:

Questions About
Mating, Birth, and Rearing

? I have read that unborn young atrophy and are not born if the mother rat is stressed out or continually disturbed. What's the purpose of that?

This phenomenon is certainly an exception, but under extreme conditions it can in fact happen that the fetuses sort of dissolve and are reabsorbed by the mother's body. This makes sense because the living conditions are so bad that the mother would have to fight for her own survival and could not successfully raise her young.

? How old should the young rats be before they are given away?

Males and females should be separated after the fourth week of life, because at eight weeks they become sexually mature and will otherwise mate with each other. Theoretically, youngsters can then be given away starting with the fifth week.

But for the healthy development of their social behavior it is better if you wait a little longer. The young males should live together for about another two weeks; the females can be kept together for a long time or stay with their mother.

? A friend's pregnant rat did not build a nest or take care of the newborns. Was she inexperienced?

The nesting instinct is inborn in female rats. If the future mother builds no nest, it may be because she can't find an appropriate place or is continually disturbed. But in both cases she will at least make an effort to gather nesting material. Inexperienced first-time mothers sometimes behave similarly. With overbred animals it happens in rare instances that they show no nest-building behavior and don't know what to do with the babies.

? Whenever our female rats are in a mood to mate, they hop around quite strangely in the cage. Is this supposed to get the males interested?

The noticeable movements and turns with the body are a part of the courtship behavior that the female uses to invite the male to follow her. After every hop, she runs away, but waits for him to follow. This little game can be repeated several times until the female finally stands still and signals with raised hind quarters that she is now ready for mating. Because the whole foreplay usually takes place during the night hours, the rat owner rarely gets to see it.

? How often can female rats have babies?

How prolific rats are is shown not only by the large number of young, but also in the number of pregnancies—up to fifteen—that a female can

experience in the course of her very short life. The best time for motherhood, with the healthiest offspring, is between the sixth and the twelfth month of life. With older females the inactive phase (diestrus) between individual periods of readiness to mate lengthens. Nature uses a "trick" to keep young rats from being born under unfavorable conditions (such as, excessively high population density): The female can store the sperm and wait for better times for the birth. With rats living in the wild this plays a particularly important role, but it's of little importance with domesticated animals.

? **Does a female choose a particular suitor when she is in heat?**
With rats there are no established couples. During the relatively short heat a female copulates several times with all the males in the group. Because male rats ejaculate sperm on only a few of their copulations, the "polygamy" increases the probability that the female will be impregnated.

? **We have three young animals at a rowdy age that romp around so wildly that we are getting concerned. How can I protect them from accidents?**
Impetuous youth is typical for rats. The youngsters measure their powers and test their physical coordination in the games of hunting and chase. However playful the scrapping may be, you can still see who has what it takes to be the boss and who is more reserved. Otherwise the youngsters have no mercy in their acrobatics and quite frequently put themselves into danger with their daredevil leaps and bold climbing. In a cage with half-grown rats you should defuse potential problem areas: The setup must not encourage big jumps, nets and hammocks under the climbing ropes and tightropes prevent freefalls, and the boards for the various floors should cover the whole width of the cage.

? **At what age can I start to give the young rats solid food?**
The mother suckles the young for around three weeks. At the end of the nursing time they start to explore their surroundings and try the first samples from the food dish. The transition to solid food is smoother and easier if you also provide some foods that are not excessively hard (mashed potatoes, yogurt).

What to Do When There Are Problems

Rats are adaptable and rarely display abnormal behaviors.
Problems usually arise only when people don't really know their
requirements and fail to provide appropriate living conditions.

Practical Tips for the Most Common Problems

In order to banish misunderstandings and difficulties from life with rats, you must know the situations and causes that have led to the undesirable behavior or put the animals into difficulties.

SEEMINGLY INSIGNIFICANT In many cases the causes and triggers of undesired behavior by rats are easily perceived. Then you can provide the needed remedy. But fairly frequently the rodents react to small, apparently minor changes in living conditions and the quality of life. And since the owner often has not considered this, in many cases it is difficult to understand the animal's strange behavior. Finally, we must also remember that every rat is its own independent personality with individual habits and preferences.

What to Do About . . . Trouble in the Pack

Situation. There are always conflicts or chases between individual group members that end only when one animal is brought to safety. From the outside it is difficult to judge how serious these conflicts are.

Cause. In an established pack, the rats know one another, and everyone knows precisely how to behave with the others. Trouble is very rare. In a new group, fighting between two equally strong animals (especially males) can last until one of them throws in the towel and

gives up. The situation is more dramatic when a new rat comes into the pack. It does not have the pack scent, is regarded as an intruder, and is attacked—and if there is no way to flee, it is seriously injured. Depending on disposition, a mother rat with nursing babies may also behave coldly toward other rats.

Remedy. If the conflict between two antagonists keeps flaring up and neither one gives up, the two opponents must be separated. But often the fights appear wilder than they really are, and peace will soon return to the pack. A new rat must never move straight in with the group; both sides need to get used to

Things are almost always peaceful in the rat pack. Still, there must be a retreat area in the cage in case an animal needs a break from group living.

each other (see page 62). As long as the young are still in the nest, the mother needs rest. "Aunts" are welcome, but intrusive animals may need to move out.

What to Do . . . with Scaredy-Cats

Situation. The rat hides as soon as the owner comes into the room; it resists

used to your smell. As soon as the rat lets itself be picked up, you can also put it under your sweater or shirt. The body warmth and the dark hiding place have a calming effect.

What to Do . . . with Biters

Situation. The rat defends itself by biting when you try to pick it up.
Cause. Bad experiences with humans and a strong territorial behavior are the most common causes for aggressiveness.

DID YOU KNOW THAT . . .

. . . a rat's circulatory system runs at top speed?

A rat's heart beats between 250 and 400 times per minute; in extreme situations (stress, panic), the heart rate can even rise to 450 beats. The breathing rate is 80 to 140 breaths per minute. At 98–100°F (36.5–37.9°C) the body temperature is only a little higher than that of humans. The high-speed circulatory system is responsible for the fact that illnesses often progress rapidly. Early diagnosis and treatment are therefore vitally important for rats.

being picked up and leaves its hideout only to get a few bites to eat and then disappears with them.
Cause. This is typical behavior of new rats that distrust everything and are afraid of strange people and unknown noises and smells. The owner has not yet tried to win the rat's trust.
Remedy. Take the house and hiding places out of the cage so that the rat can no longer creep away, and begin trust training (see page 58). Put a piece of clothing you have worn (socks or a glove) into the cage to get the animal

But if a previously peaceful animal becomes nippy when you try to pick it up, it is almost always a sign that it doesn't feel good and is in pain that is aggravated by touch.
Remedy. Wrap your hand with a fabric that can withstand the teeth, and put a worn sock over it (containing your smell). The behavior generally drops off as soon as the rat notices that its bites have no visible effect. With fearful biters, trust-building measures are necessary. A veterinarian must investigate pain caused by touch.

Most problem situations can be avoided
by earning the rat's trust so that
it spontaneously seeks its owner's company.

What to Do . . . with Notorious Escape Artists

Situation. The rat uses every weak spot in the cage and forces itself through the tiniest cracks and openings to go out on discovery tours.

Cause. Rats are curious creatures, and they have amazing physical strength and a strong urge to explore. A cage door that is not properly secured or a loose food hatch can be concealed from them for only a short time, and then they will be worked at until they give way.

Remedy. When you buy a cage, look for doors that fit precisely and close securely. Reinforce simple hook or spring clasps with a padlock. With adult rats the space between the bars should not exceed about ½ inch (1 cm) (7⁄16 inch/12 mm would be better); with young animals, no more than about ⅜ inch (10 mm). For them a tight wire mesh attached to the inside of the cage bars is recommended.

What to Do . . . When a Rat Vanishes

Situation. While the rats are outside the cage, one rat disappears from the scene—and you don't know where it is hiding.

Cause. The parolees are interested in every crack and every dark corner. Many rats settle into a particularly cozy hiding place and don't even think about returning to the cage at the appointed hour.

Remedy. Eliminate this type of hiding place and rat-proof the room (see page 60). With these measures a missing rat can be lured out of its hiding place.

▸ Hold treats in front of the suspected hiding places. Because the rodents are always fed after their excursions outside the cage, in most cases the growling stomach will win out over the appeal of cave life.

▸ If the offering is scorned, or if the rat's whereabouts cannot be deduced, put some treats in the center of the room (maybe even in another house) and temporarily leave the room. Good choices are foods that the rat has to eat on the spot (mashed potatoes, yogurt) and cannot drag back to the hiding place.

. . . and out it goes:
Rats will discover
every weak spot
and hole in
the cage.
▼

▶ If the creature still remains lost, put some more treats into the house, spread flour around the feeding spot, and wait until the next morning. Usually the rat will venture forth to eat during the night, and its tracks will reveal the hiding place.

▶ With a particularly well-concealed refugee, unfortunately sometimes the only thing that can be done is move the furniture around.

What to Do . . . in Case of Birthing Difficulties

Situation. Giving birth to the young is taking significantly longer than an hour, the mother is visibly exhausted, and the breaks between individual births keep getting longer.

Cause. A mother rat generally has six to twelve, but also frequently more (in exceptional cases up to twenty) young. Especially young and inexperienced mothers reach their physical limits with a large number of newborns, so they ultimately don't have the strength to give birth to all of the babies.

Remedy. With experienced mothers, birthing problems are rare; with very young mothers giving birth for the first time, you should make sure before the birth that your veterinarian can be reached in an emergency. Notify the veterinarian immediately if the birthing takes excessively long or involves unforeseen complications.

What to Do . . . with Unexpected Reproduction

Situation. A female gives birth unexpectedly and without planning. In many cases the owner notices the undesired pregnancy only a few days before the birth.

Cause. The female is pregnant because the young animals were not segregated by sex soon enough; when females and unneutered males are kept together, undesired reproduction is the result; in buying a female it was not noticed that she was already pregnant.

Remedy. As a rat owner you should make sure that the offspring end up only in good hands. Your veterinarian, animal welfare agencies, and rat clubs will provide additional help. Some associations have set up a placement data bank that you can visit on the Internet (see addresses on page 141). In addition, on many other Internet sites, experienced rat owners and rat aficionados will help you with valuable

◀ *A brave patient: Not every rat takes its medicine so willingly. But you can use some small tricks to reach the goal (see facing page).*

practical tips and important contact addresses.

What to Do . . . If a Rat Doesn't Take Its Medicine

Situation. Pills that are smuggled in with the food often are left untouched; liquid medicines get swallowed only if they taste good.
Cause. Rats are selective eaters. Even though domesticated animals are less suspicious than wild rats, they are quick to sort out strange and less tasty pieces of food in the food dish.
Remedy. Crush up pills into powder and mix it in with cottage cheese, baby food, yogurt, or mashed fruit to hide the taste of the medication. Drops that the rat refuses to take straight from the dropper can also be mixed in with mashed potatoes or cottage cheese. Sometimes it also helps to mix it in with some marmalade. Alternatively, you can dribble it onto zwieback (or a cracker), which will quickly soak up the fluid. Ask your veterinarian for additional doses of medication for trial and error of mixing medication with food.

What to Do . . . When Visitors Arrive

Situation. Visitors are unexpectedly confronted by rats running free in the room, react coolly and indignantly, or even experience panic.
Cause. People who don't know rats have very different reactions to direct contact—even if they are not afraid of animals.
Remedy. When visitors come, keep the rats inside the cage. If the guests are interested in the rodents, that's the best

---

Common Behavioral Problems

In most instances behavior abnormalities in rats are caused by improper living conditions.

○ Aggression in the pack directed toward new rats; sometimes between equally strong males.

○ Aggressive behavior directed toward the owner by animals that are shy and not yet acclimated: territorial defense.

○ Apathy in subordinated pack animals; often also a sign of serious illness.

○ Biting from insecurity, fear, or pain. Gentle nibbles are a gesture of affection.

○ Refusal to eat when sick.

○ Intolerance of other pack members on the part of old and weak animals.

○ Self-destructive behavior (scratching, licking fur) with parasite infestation, stress, stereotypies.

○ Stereotypies (see page 132).

○ Restlessness and excessive motor activity under stress, parasite infestation, panic.

○ Creeping away in the case of animals that are fearful or not yet acclimated.

○ Sharpening the teeth under fear, aggression, pain; but can also be a manifestation of well-being.

... and suddenly there are more important things

For many months the children have cared for their rats with lots of devotion and love. But as they grow older, they develop new interests and neglect the care of the animals. If necessary, the parents have to step in so that the cage dwellers don't get shortchanged.

WHEN INTEREST WANES For a long time the children and the rats were fast friends. The rodents were the focus of the children's world; they were the topic of conversation with friends and were the best playmates of all. But now the growing children are discovering many other exciting things.

Children Grow Up

It is a difficult time for the whole family when the youngsters outgrow their children's shoes and reach puberty. Now they want to be taken seriously as adults, and they react with defiance and rebellion if they are treated as children. Even the best childhood games are suddenly taboo— and sometimes this also applies to animal friends. The adolescents find it painful when they have to be bothered with kids' stuff.

A Hard Line Helps No One

Commands, grounding, and withholding privileges don't have much effect. On the contrary: Browbeating your children into taking care of the animals against their will only strengthens their resistance. The cage dwellers are the ones who will suffer from this.

A Conversation Between Adults

People who respect their interests and the needs of their children and treat them as adults on an equal footing have already won half the battle. They can also appeal to their sense of responsibility and their duty to the rats. Allow your children a separate monthly budget that they can manage independently and use for all expenditures for the care of their charges.

Rats at a Mouse Click

Nowadays the computer and Internet are of course an important part of life for children and adolescents. This can also be used to keep up or reawaken the interest in the pets. There are countless pages on the Internet that deal with small mammals, and with rats in particular. Many links entice youngsters to journeys of discovery in the adventurous world of rodents. The children can exchange and pick up many practical tips from other rat owners in chat rooms. It's really neat if they have their own home page that they can design themselves and on which they can introduce their rats to the Internet community.

place for the people to observe them. In the safety of their home, the animals will also show themselves to be much more receptive and confident in the presence of the strangers.

What to Do . . . If the Neighbors Protest

Situation. The neighbors have found out that you have rats. They complain to the landlord and pressure him to prohibit ownership.
Cause. Rats have always had a bad image. Many people find them disgusting and fear that the rodents will nest everywhere and spread diseases.
Remedy. Precedents are clear: There is no annoyance to the other residents as a result of rats in the house (see page 57). Speak with the other tenants to give them an understanding of the nature and the behavior of the animals and eliminate fear and prejudices.

What to Do . . . If You Have to Move

Situation. After moving to a different house the rats are shy and nervous.
Cause. The strange surroundings make the rats feel insecure; when they are outside the cage they find none of their familiar markings.
Remedy. In the first few days, leave the rats inside the cage, until they have gotten used to the unknown smells and noises. At first restrict their exercise outside the cage to a small area.

After a move it ▶ takes time for the rats to get used to the new surroundings. Close contact with the trusted human is especially important at this time.

How Can Stereotypies Be Avoided?

Situation. A rat continually repeats the same movements and behaviors. Many animals also are inclined to gnaw repeatedly on the bars of the cage.

Cause. Behaviors that are repeated, follow the same pattern, and are not purposeful are known as stereotypies. "Driving in neutral" is characteristic of animals that don't get enough exercise or have nothing to do. Stereotypies manifest themselves in various forms, such as in continually licking the fur, swinging the head, or chasing the tail. Often the action is like an addiction and can trigger illnesses or serious behavior abnormalities.

Remedy. Rats are demanding creatures that need continual challenges for body and mind. Opportunities to play and keep busy inside the cage, time outside the cage every day, and intensive contact with a human protect behaviors from stereotypies.

TIP

Love Signals with the Ears

Even many rat owners with years of experience don't know what it means when a rat rapidly moves its ears back and forth. The other rats in the cage understand this signal much more clearly: A rat that wiggles its ears is walking the path of love and is clearly communicating its readiness to mate.

When Rats Grow Older

Many rats live to be five or six years old, but the average life expectancy of domesticated animals is between two and three years—still greater than that of their relatives living in the wild. Visible signs of aging usually appear starting with the fifteenth month of life, but sometimes even sooner. With older animals, the fondness for exercise decreases and the susceptibility to infectious diseases increases. Wounds also take longer to heal.

Physical Signs of Age

- General: Older rats appear less athletic overall; their stomach is no longer round, the sides are often sunken, and their sitting posture is more bent than that of younger animals. In very old rats thoracic flank respiration is typical.
- Fur: Increasingly unkempt, especially when grooming is neglected.
- Skin: More susceptible to scab formation, eczema, tumors, and other tissue changes.
- Eyes: Clouding of the lens, diminished vision up to complete blindness.
- Mouth and throat: Increased susceptibility to infections and sores.
- Teeth: Excessive growth of the rodent teeth if the animals take in less hard food and don't wear down the teeth enough; also often the result of infections in the pharyngeal space.
- Claws: They don't get worn down enough because of the rat's reduced activity.
- Body weight: Weight loss with decreasing appetite and incomplete nutritional utilization.

A landscape with lots of ways to keep busy protects against stereotypies (see facing page).

Behavioral Changes with Age

▶ Mobility: The desire for movement decreases; older animals play and climb less frequently and often pass up the excursions outside the cage.
▶ Curiosity: Many seniors cease showing interest in changes in the cage and new toys, and come less frequently to greet people at the cage bars.
▶ Group living: Continuous contact with younger and more active rats is a strain; old rats pull back more frequently from the group.
▶ Tolerance: Older rats usually respond less tolerantly than younger animals to disturbances from other rats or people during their rest periods and while they are eating. Depending on their disposition, this can even lead to aggressive behavior and defensive biting.

▶ Recovery phases: the sleep and rest periods grow longer.
▶ Contact behavior: Many older animals become more affectionate and seek out the owner more frequently, but others keep their distance.
▶ Food intake: Loss of appetite is a typical symptom in old animals. In many instances reduced fluid intake is even more serious. This puts a major strain on the animal and poses a great health risk.
▶ Reproduction: In older mothers there is a heightened risk of stillbirths and other birthing problems. In addition the females find rearing the young to be too taxing.

MY PET

Is My Rat Old?

With many rats the first signs of aging appear in the fifteenth month of life. But there are great differences among individuals. With these tests you can find out which of your rats have reached their senior years.

The Test Begins

○ Activity: Does the rat go upstairs using the steps more frequently than the rope?
○ Curiosity: Is its interest in new toys and other objects in the cage declining?
○ Contact: Does the rat no longer come to the cage bars to greet you right away?
○ Need for rest: Does the rat stay in its sleeping house longer and more frequently than before?
○ Group living: Does the rat stay away from its colleagues more frequently?

My Test Results:

With Lots of Love and Care

Here's how to make a rat's life easier and make sure it is happy with you and remains healthy into old age:

▸ Cuddling: Many older animals need close contact with a human and are "addicted" to cuddling.
▸ Fitness sleep: Now disturbances during the rest periods absolutely must be avoided. Provide an extra sleeping house for the seniors.
▸ Eating and drinking: Place additional food and water bowls in appropriate places in the cage.
▸ Security: Knots in the climbing rope make it easier to climb up; nets under tightropes and railings on stairs protect against falls.

▸ Stress-free: Protect the old-timers from hustle and bustle and loud noises; don't continually fuss around with the cage.
▸ Familiar surroundings: Frequently moving or changing the furnishings makes old animals feel much more insecure than it does young ones.
▸ Saying goodbye: When an older rat does nothing but sit apathetically in a corner, clearly in pain, you should not prolong its suffering. Have it put to sleep by a veterinarian.

All eyes, ears, and nose: With their sharp sense perceptions, rats react to everything that goes on in their environment. ▸

Animal Sitter's Guidelines

You want to take a vacation and a pet sitter will take care of your little friends. On this page you can write down everything that your vacation replacement needs to know. That way your rats will get the best care and you can enjoy your vacation to the fullest and with a clear conscience!

My rats' names are:

They look like this:

Things they like to eat:

This amount every day:

This amount once every week:

Between-meal snacks:

What they drink:

The right feeding times:

Where the food is kept:

Housecleaning:

This gets cleaned every day:

This gets cleaned weekly:

They like this TLC:

Neat ways to keep them busy:

Things they don't like:

Things my rats are not allowed to do:

Another important thing:

This is their veterinarian:

My vacation address and phone number:

INDEX

Page numbers in **bold** print
refer to illustrations.

ASSOCIATIONS AND CLUBS

American Fancy Rat and Mouse Association (AFRMA); *www.afrma.org;* since 1983, a nonprofit international organization that encourages breeding and exhibition of fancy rats for show and pets, plus the education of the public about the qualities of these animals

Rat and Mouse Club of America
55 Valley View Drive
Fitchburg, MA 01420-2138
webmaster@rmca.org

Michigan Fancy Rat Association;
mifancyrat.org; dedicated to educating the public about what wonderful animals fancy rats are

Great Lakes Fancy Rat Association;
www.glfra.com; dedicated to promoting fancy rats as the wonderful companion animals that they are

California Association of Rat Enthusiasts (CARE); *http://careratclub.com;* since 2006, dedicated to educating breeders, owners, and the general public about pet rats

Association of Colorado Rat Enthusiasts (ACRE); *http://acrecoloradoratclub.org;* an educational rat forum and an affiliate of the American Fancy Rat and Mouse Association

LilRatscals Rattery and Home of the Canadian Pet Rat Club; *www.lilratscal.com;* an electronic message board for rat enthusiasts

Locating small-animal veterinarians with experience treating rodents: There are countless resources online and in the yellow pages of most telephone directories. Before becoming a pet rat owner, identify the veterinarians in your area and query them about their experience in dealing with rats.

Questions about keeping pet rats: Your pet shop, local veterinarian, rat clubs and associations, animal shelters, humane societies, and Internet resources can provide guidance and answers.

On the Internet: A search on *pet rats* or more specific topics will produce many hits; some of these sites offer a question-and-answer service involving experienced rat owners.

Sources of rats: Local pet shops, rat clubs, Internet sites, animal shelters, and humane societies; also check the bulletin board at your veterinarian's practice and the pet section of classified ads in local newspapers.

PERIODICALS

Rat and Mouse Gazette
55 Valley View Drive
Fitchburg, MA 01420-2138
(Visit *http://wererat.net/rmca.htm* for some excerpts previously published.)

Rats Magazine
www.afrma.org/sales/ratsmag.htm

HELPFUL BOOKS

Bulla, Gisela. *Fancy Rats: A Complete Pet Owner's Manual.* Hauppauge, NY: Barron's Educational Series, 1998.

Buscis, Gerry and Barbara Somerville. *Training Your Pet Rat.* Hauppauge, NY: Barron's Educational Series, 2000.

Cardinal, Ginger. *The Rat: An Owner's Guide to a Happy, Healthy Pet.* Howell Book House, 1997.

Ducommun, Debbie. *Rats: Complete Care Guide.* Bow Tie Press, 2002.

___. *The Complete Guide to Rat Training: Tricks and Games for Rat Fun and Fitness.* Neptune City, NJ: TFH Publications, 2008.

Himsel, Carol A., DVM. *Rats: A Complete Pet Owner's Manual.* Hauppauge, NY: Barron's Educational Series, 1991.

Mays, Nick. *Your First Fancy Rat.* Neptune City, NJ: TFH Publications, 1996.

Patterson, Colin. *Pet Rats.* Lulu.com, 2006.

PHOTOS

The pictures on the front and back covers and inside are as follows:

Front cover: gray-white check

Outside front cover flap: top, young gray-white check; lower: cinnamon

Inside front cover: left page: top right, gray-white check; circle: bareback; lower left: husky; right page: upper left: two young gray-white checks; circle: husky; lower left: dark gray self; lower right: husky and gray-white checks

Outside rear cover flap: the author, Gerd Ludwig

Inside rear cover flap (from left to right): bareback, two young huskies, gray-white check, black-eyed white

Back cover: gray-white check

Inside: p. 6: young husky; p. 30: young husky and young gray-white check; p. 48: young cream self; page 66: gray-white checks and hooded (middle); p. 78: husky and gray-white checks; p. 96: gray-white check; p. 112: young bareback; p. 124: husky (standing) and gray-white check

Important Notice

Dealing with rats can result in injuries from bites and scratches that must be treated by a doctor. If you are allergic to animal hair, you must consult with your doctor before buying a rat. When the rats are running around free in the house, avoid life-threatening electric shock by making sure there are no exposed electrical cords that the rodents could gnaw.

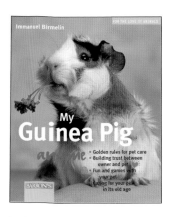

The Author

Dr. Gerd Ludwig is a freelance journalist and zoologist. He has written practical handbooks on dogs, cats, and rats for Gräfe und Unzer Publishers.

The Photographer

Regina Kuhn is a freelance photo designer and has worked for many years as a pet photographer. Her animal books appear in many well-known book publishers and periodicals. In addition she works in calendar and advertising production.

All photos in this book are by Regina Kuhn, except for Getty: p. 8-1, 8-2, 9, 11.

Acknowledgment

The author and publisher thank Prof. Harald Schliemann, Hamburg, for detailed information and proofing the information on rat biology.

The publisher and photographer thank the following for their support: Rebekka Lehmann, Herleshausen; Camilla Kruidbos, Saasveld; Annika Schulz, Herleshausen; Tierzucht (Animal Breeding) Renate Triesch, Zaunroeden; Zoo and Angler Center, Eisenach.

The title of the German book is *Meine Ratte*
English translation by Eric Bye

All inquiries should be addressed to:
Barron's Educational Series, Inc.
250 Wireless Boulevard
Hauppauge, NY 11788
www.barronseduc.com

Library of Congress Catalog Card No.: 2009033313

ISBN-13: 978-0-7641-4431-8
ISBN-10: 0-7641-4431-6

Library of Congress Cataloging-in-Publication Data

Ludwig, Gerd.
 [Meine Ratte. English]
 My rat/ Gerd Ludwig.
   p. cm.
 Includes bibliographical references and index.
 ISBN-13: 978-0-7641-4431-8 (alk. paper)
 ISBN-10: 0-7641-4431-6 (alk. paper)
 1. Rats as pets. I. Title.
 SF459.R3L8313 2010
 636.935'2—dc22   2009033313

Printed in China
9 8 7 6 5 4 3 2 1